ESTHER

A Play

(Inspired by the biblical story of Esther)

PHILIP BEGHO

Monarch Books

ESTHER

First Published 2002

copyright © **Philip Begho**
All rights reserved

All rights in this play are strictly reserved. No performance or reading of the play may be given and no copy of the play or any part thereof may be reproduced, stored in a retrieval system, or transmitted in any form or by means, electronic, mechanical, photocopying, recording, or otherwise, without the prior written permission of the author, with the exception of brief excerpts in magazines, articles, reviews, etc.

All applications regarding the rights to this play (whether performing or otherwise) should be made to the author through his publishers.

Email: monarch_books@yahoo.com
Tel: +234 8060069597

ISBN 978-32224-3-0

PUBLISHED BY MONARCH BOOKS
NIGERIA

ESTHER

CHARACTERS

KING AHASUERUS, Ruler of the Persian Empire.

MORDECAI, A Jew, porter at the king's gate.

ESTHER, His daughter.

NATHAN, A Jew, Mordecai's friend.

HAMAN, A merchant of immense wealth.

ZERESH, His wife.

BIGTHANA, Chief of the king's guard.

TEREZ, His deputy.

BILBO
SIKURU
MIHESO   } Haman's servants.
1st BOY
2nd BOY

HATHACH
                  } Queen's guards.
MANSUR

HALALISA
LEILA   }   Queen's maids.
LOLITHE

HARBONA
                }   King's attendants.
ZETHAR

ASHANTI
JABUL   }   King's guards.
ASHKENAZ

HEGAI, Keeper of the king's harem.

MEMUCAN, One of the king's Seven Advisers.

TABRIZ, A General in the Persian army.

AMOS, A Jew, with business dealings in the palace.

A PHYSICIAN.

1st ROYAL ESCORT.
2nd ROYAL ESCORT.
3rd ROYAL ESCORT.

Nobles, Advisers, Generals, Guards, Eunuchs, Attendants, Servants, Acrobats, Entertainers, Musicians, Scribes, Suitors.

SCENE: Susa, royal seat of the Persian Empire.
                     About 480BC.

Act One

Scene 1.—MORDECAI'S *house. The living room.*

ESTHER *is frantically looking for a hiding place as she hears* MORDECAI *returning home.*

MORDECAI [*offstage*]: Esther…!
[*Enter* MORDECAI *as* ESTHER *slips from view.*]
Esther…
[*He peeps into the kitchen.*]
Hadassah, child…
[*He pokes his head round other doors.*]
Daughter… Esther… Daughter…
[*He goes to the front door, opens it slightly and calls.*]
Esther! … Esther!
[*He listens but there is no response. Leaving the door ajar he returns bewildered to the living room. Suddenly, with a flourish,* ESTHER *emerges.*]

ESTHER: Ta-ra! Ta-ra! All hail the Queen!
[*Laughing, she hugs her father.*]

MORDECAI: Is this how you treat your father?
[*Enter* NATHAN.]

NATHAN [*mimicking* MORDECAI]: Esther! Esther!

Had she stood with pin-points for ears
At the ends of Persia's farthest fields,
Yet would your cries have felled her, Mordecai.

ESTHER [*hugging* NATHAN]:
Did worry ever so quickly forge
A furrowed mask on any girl's father?
I think not, Uncle Nathan; no...

MORDECAI:
Worry comes easy to those who know
The sons of Haman are loose in Susa.

NATHAN:
The ochre stains at the square's marbled font
Speak of Reuben's flogging, they say.

MORDECAI:
The sons of Haman the very culprits.
But 'twas a soft piece of their villainy this day,
For they seized Tamar, and to see her now –
The poor maid! Maid no more.

NATHAN: Pedahzur's daughter?

MORDECAI:
She. The gate was abuzz with the tale:
A sorry day – while you did feast.

NATHAN: Can Haman do nothing?
Can the man not rear his cubs to leash?

MORDECAI: The man himself
Is the secret spring that waters the poison-herbs.
Be not deceived by his honeyed slavering;
His tongue is the very sceptre of dissemblance.

NATHAN:
The more reason then, Mordecai, to yield
Soft and willing ear to my exhortations.

ESTHER:
But why do they sport so cruelly with us? Why?

NATHAN:
No season this for whys and pained wherefores,
But time that begs us bend and steer our feet
To paths that beat a homebound trail.
Mordecai, will you for ever shut off reason?

ESTHER:
And now I smell a storm – time for dinner!

NATHAN: I shall eat nothing, child.

ESTHER [*laughing*]:
As the stars shall hide their glow…
                [*Exit to the kitchen.*

[MORDECAI *and* NATHAN *lounge around a dining table.*]

NATHAN: Mordecai…

MORDECAI: Nathan?

NATHAN: Does it not rankle you, this thing?

MORDECAI: The Jew-baiting?

NATHAN:
No; this wears no such raucous robe
But hides its venom in velvet folds.

MORDECAI: What is it?
[*Re-enter* ESTHER *with wine. She serves.*]

NATHAN:
Of the men in scented chambers feasting
With the king now in closing fête, not one
Is Jew. No forehead there spells itself Jew.

MORDECAI:
And no Jew would wish it, could they, like me,
Slouch easy at Esther's contenting table.

ESTHER [*starting off to the kitchen*]:
And with the wine comes something most tasty.

NATHAN [*stopping her*]:
Truly, Esther, what would move me eat again?

MORDECAI:
The king's banquet has done this thing, Esther.
While I with menacing tales of Haman's sons
Did at my post contend, your worthy uncle,
Man of valour as he is, did tussle brave
With the king's meats to win a rounded belly.
[*They laugh,* ESTHER *sitting.*]

NATHAN: In the garden of the rabble.

MORDECAI:
In scented chambers or rabble gardens
The king's meat is the king's meat –

ESTHER:
And a rounded belly gleams as valiant.
[*They laugh.*]
Did you see the queen, Uncle Nathan?
Does her beauty run as true as fame relates?

NATHAN:
None is more beautiful than she, they say
Who have not seen you, Esther.

ESTHER: Uncle!
 [*Exits, bashfully, to the kitchen.*

NATHAN:
Modesty that blinds one to one's beauty
Is the crown that adorns truest beauty.
Mordecai, for the sake of Esther's happiness,
Leave this land and come home with me.

MORDECAI:
If I profess to know a thing, it's this:
Esther, content and happy in Persia,
Will in Persia prosper.

NATHAN: Content – unwed? Happy?

MORDECAI: Hush! I hear her.
[*Re-enter* ESTHER *with a laden tray.*]

NATHAN [*surveying the tray*]: Esther!
Now have you proved this stomach inconstant –
Menaced to expansion by your stove's delights!

ESTHER [*placing tray on table*]:
Expand stomach then to double increase:
More lies a pace away.
[*Exit again to kitchen.*

NATHAN:
He's a favoured man you find your daughter.

MORDECAI: I find no one.
[*Re-enter* ESTHER *unnoticed, listening by the door.*]
She will marry whom she will marry.

NATHAN: Do you jest?

MORDECAI:
The one duty I shall never perform
Is throw her to the locks of arms unloved.

NATHAN: But you jest…

MORDECAI: She will marry as love leads.

NATHAN: Love…

MORDECAI: Love.

NATHAN:
Wisdom has died, has died in you, Mordecai.
You know full well grave danger sniffs hot
Upon the heels of great beauty unwed –
Or perhaps you know it no more, having lost
All knowing since this madness teemed leaf in you…
[*He notices* ESTHER.]
Esther, if your father in his duty flags…
But what tears are these? Esther…
[ESTHER, *tearfully, withdraws to the kitchen.*]
[*To* MORDECAI] She weeps…
[*Lights fade.*]

Scene 2.—*The King's palace. His banquet chamber.*

KING AHASUERUS, *Courtiers and Guests in feast. Performing Acrobats pull in a chest containing gold articles which they distribute to astonished Guests. The royal gong is sounded. A hush. The King rises to speak.*

GUESTS:
Live for ever, King Ahasuerus!
Live for ever, O great king!

KING AHASUERUS:
The finest gold for you, princes of my delight!
Friends of my joy, golden Ophir's fairest offerings!
Yet is finest gold unbrooched by purest gem flawed;
Therefore shall we unflaw the king's bounty
And to the gaze of eyes disclose his rarest gem.
[*To two attending Eunuchs*] Harbona! Zethar!

HARBONA & ZETHAR:
Live for ever, O King Ahasuerus!

KING AHASUERUS:
Fetch hither the king's jewel!
The dawn with trysting eyes does oft with haste arise
To gaze on tender Vashti's flawless form.
Fetch then my jewel! Bring forth the queen!
[*Pause.*]
[*To Attendants*] Why do you gasp? And you, my princes,
Why do your breaths suckle the air in sorry squeak?
[*To the two Attendants*] But go! Go!

Act One

HARBONA & ZETHAR: As the king commands.
>   [*Exeunt.*

KING AHASUERUS [*to Guests*]:
Your minds question, apprehension rears.
So none ever before has done this thing;
But none before was Ahasuerus.
Ahasuerus may do all he pleases,
For he is Ahasuerus, King of Persia.
And Vashti is but Vashti – a jewel,
But a woman still. And I – Ahasuerus.
Solomon of old, like Ahasuerus,
Had riches to outgleam the silver stars.
But did Solomon, like Ahasuerus,
Ever lay table to feast the gaping world?
Of whom have you heard it told, what emperor,
What monarch, what king, of what ruler
Have you heard it said did unlock his bounty
To all, high-born or low, slave or free,
In revel to crown days of feasting
Topping a hundred by almost a hundred?
Now let all drink; drink joyously the king's wine!
Sup and drink all in this crowning night of cheer,
While these quick-limbed sons of lately rebelled
    Egypt
Do here cavort and disport to our heart's content.
Nor could their leaping limbs and prancing skills
Avail them aught against Persia's avenging wrath
As with arms of thundering steel we fell on them,

And they fell and fell as all will fall who think
To lift the knee from Ahasuerus's sprawling earth!
But cavort on, cavorters; revel on, revellers;
Drink on, drinkers – oil your eyes with wine,
The king's jewel soon comes to trance your
    swimming gaze!

[*He sits. Performers entertain. Laughter and revelling. At length there is the sound of approach. All eyes turn to the door. Re-enter Eunuchs without the queen.*]

KING AHASUERUS: I glimpse not the queen!

HARBONA: Great king…

KING AHASUERUS: Speak!

HARBONA:
May it please the king far from the general ear
Hear his servants?

KING AHASUERUS:
Unload your words here! Speak!

HARBONA: O king…

KING AHASUERUS: Speak!

HARBONA: O noble king…

KING AHASUERUS:
Speak! Lest I slip my knife to slip your tongue!

HARBONA: O king, the queen will not come.
[*Silence. The King's eyes travel to* ZETHAR.]

ZETHAR [*bowed by royal gaze*]:
It is as Harbona speaks, my king.

KING AHASUERUS:
Did she possessed of tongue not proffer speech?

ZETHAR:
Thus spoke she: 'I disdain these flighty janglings.
Should Persia's queen to wind and fancy flutter?
I jangle nowhere, nor ever dangle more.'
[*Silence. The King glares at the two Eunuchs who then lower themselves beneath his gaze, finally lying prostrate. Amidst continued silence, the King returns to his seat where he remains awhile in stunned unease.*]

KING AHASUERUS [*to the two Attendants*]: Go…

HARBONA & ZETHAR: Live for ever, O king!
[*They return to their posts.*]

KING AHASUERUS [*to his group of Seven Advisers*]:
Princes Seven, you who counsel the king,
This profligacy of feline madness
Has not been sealed from you; counsel me, therefore,
Onto wisdom's highway, its law-encrusted paths,
That the law, mightier than a storm of queens,

May blaze with strong unshuttered rays.
[*Silence.*]
Will none speak?

MEMUCAN [*rising*]:
Ahasuerus – No greater king is there!

KING AHASUERUS:
Memucan, heart of wisdom, speak.

MEMUCAN:
Rebellion is but born to be crushed;
It cannot hide in royal robes and snarl.
It is rebellion though clad in silken garb;
Rebellion, consigned to the short-lived day.
Queen Vashti's deed slurs not the king alone
But all men, exalted or beggarly low.
It is the firebrand to kindle in women
Wicked embers of smouldering defiance.
What fate is a man's whose gate will not lock?
What fate a city's whose walls do mutiny breathe?
Let the king therefore with no leave of further stay
Give the law swift motion, and in iron ribs
Of terms unalterable, to where no wind
Or fancy flutters, banish the rebel queen.
[*He sits amid a hushed murmur of approval.*]
[*Pause.*]

KING AHASUERUS: So let it be.

As noble Memucan has spoken, let it be.
She shall jangle nowhere, nor ever dangle more.
[*To his chief bodyguard*] Bigthana!

BIGTHANA: Live for ever, O king!

KING AHASUERUS: Terez!

TEREZ: O king, live for ever!

KING AHASUERUS:
Worthy guards, my foremost bucklers;
You who have shielded me from dangers past,
Now go to Vashti, who, as I speak,
No more is queen, and shield her from dangers
By the king's ungentle wrath disgorged, lest I,
Straying from Memucan's restraining counsel,
Do with bitter sword upon her fall,
Who once the royal palm of monarchy did tend.

BIGTHANA & TEREZ: As the king commands.
[*Exeunt.*

KING AHASUERUS: But stay the men!

HARBONA [*by the door*]: Bigthana! Terez!
[*The men return, pay homage, and await orders. The King stares at them, then his hands fly to his temple as though in pain. He gazes at the men, then at his hands.*]

KING AHASUERUS:
For her silken throat… But go! Go!
        [*Exeunt* BIGTHANA *and* TEREZ.
[HAMAN *rises from his seat and throws himself at the feet of the King.*]

HAMAN:
Ahasuerus – No greater king is there!
Live for ever! Live for ever, mightiest emperor,
Ruling the unsearchable earth! Live for ever,
Emperor whose name streaks the lofty skies
With blinding silver sear! Live for ever!
[*Silence.*]

KING AHASUERUS: Rise!
Your face reveals not itself to our remembrance.
[HAMAN *rises.*]

HAMAN:
Greatest of kings, live for ever!
I am Haman son of humble Hammedatha,
With free blood of Agagite flowing.

KING AHASUERUS:
Haman? Do I now meet the man whose name,
Enveined deep in marbled slates and trading decks,
Long has rung where gold and silver long resound?

HAMAN:
A humble merchant, O king, am I,
And your humble servant.

KING AHASUERUS:
What then, humble merchant-servant, would you
    speak?

HAMAN:
To behold your face, O king, at close approach
Was a dream that besieged me till I found means
To slip into your banquet of favoured princes.
And now that I have seen the king's face
I dread no more the yielding of this flesh
To decay, nor fear the closing of day.
Your bounty, O king, is voiced earthwide by golden
    deeds;
Do all men not know it?
I, like prince and courtier here, with trancèd eye,
Have seen the golden depths of royal breast
And do still float in eddies of delight.
And as for the king's might, it twins his bounty:
In vassal glitter and chains of opulent thrones
Stretching the backs of sprawling nations,
Tremoring the very stars to fearful homage.
Do all men not know it?
They know it, and their hearts with wonder throb.
All men know the king's bounty, his awesome might,
But do all men know this thing which I, today,

In this place, with marvel-sodden eyes have seen?
For though these eyes have gazed upon the king,
Where men have seen the king, not so these eyes.
They have gazed and seen virtue's own sire,
Virtue's fount, the very spring of virtue;
And on his brow what name bears he but Mercy?
Mercy today has walked the onyx of these floors,
And graced this day the cedars of these walls,
And in walking his course has met Justice,
And Justice to Mercy has bowed the knee
As lesser virtue always to greater will bow.
For Justice did decree Queen Vashti's death,
But Mercy said 'Not so,' and Mercy did prevail.
O most worthy king – who with streaming light
Of purest virtue has blazed me blind
And from my tongue wrung praise so deeply drawn
It empties its vault now of every strength
And wilts me down at Virtue's feet!
[*He falls prostrate before the King.*]
[*Silence.*]

KING AHASUERUS:
Who was it, Haman, sent you to disperse from me
My gathering gloom? Who was it sent you?
And how well you have done it; how so well!
[*Pause.*]

                                        Rise now!
Rise, who fell before me a humble merchant;
Rise now a prince! And loop yourself firm

To our court, favoured of favoured courtiers.
[HAMAN *rises.*]
And having grasped our favour, cling not only
To honour's rungs but climb onto our bosom heart;
And as token thereof, as mark of friendship,
Ask of me now a desire, and it is yours.

HAMAN:
To see the king's face is honour enough,
To stand favoured in his sight is surfeit friendship.

KING AHASUERUS:
As all men know, I think it pleasing
To please in pleasing ways all who please me,
Therefore yet ask of me a pleasing token.

HAMAN:
As the king wills, this is my desire:
Not tarrying, a new queen, whose sight and manner
Ever will glad the king, be sought and found.
Only he who never has known love's true embrace
Will snuggle to arms that hug less than deep.
And as token to which my lord has urged,
This I ask: Let the king in private chambers,
Away from other ears, give ear to a thought
Whose blossoming, I vouch, will yield Persia her
   queen.

KING AHASUERUS:
Lord Haman, worthy prince!
Storing up royal rewards by silken sacks!
In accord, hie we then to some quiet chamber
Where you may at ease unravel me your thoughts.
Memucan! Princes of Persia! Royal scribes!
Do all, with haste, as may with strong gust
Trumpet the fall from grace of Vashti.
Up now and about! Rouse yourselves to deeds!
                    [*Exeunt the King and* HAMAN.
[*The chamber bustles. Lights fade.*]

Scene 3.—*A secluded place in the palace.*

BIGTHANA *and* TEREZ *on their way to Queen Vashti.* TEREZ *suddenly stops.*

TEREZ: Bigthana, what now?

BIGTHANA: What nettles you so?

TEREZ:
Has calamity, robbing you of freedom,
Robbed you, too, of your wits?

BIGTHANA:
My freedom is unscathed; it knows no scratch
Nor fears a scritch. The days tread surely
Towards Liberty's gate. Nothing has changed that.

TEREZ:
Calamity truly has claimed your wits
And oafed you fat. You go to snuff the freedom
Of she who promised us freedom, and cannot see
That in the annulment of hers, we lose
The promise of ours.

BIGTHANA:
The words of kings and queens outlive their flesh;
Though Vashti falls, her word stands to bind the king
In the fetters loosed from our slavish limbs.
A few more days, Terez, a few days,
And freedom garlands us true.

TEREZ: And if the king should balk?

BIGTHANA: He cannot balk.

TEREZ: But if he should?

BIGTHANA:
He will not! We shall not go to him unclothed,
But will cover our approach in the pleading
Of one esteemed, who, having the king's ear,
And having lips strong to bend the lofty cedar
To lowly cowslip stoop, will with ease bend the king
To our fair and worthy cause.

TEREZ:
When he did utter the queen's banishment,
My dagger, full jealous for my freedom,
Leapt in my hand and raged, thirsting deep
For his rabid heart.

BIGTHANA:
Let patience slake your thirst. My soul pants no less
Than yours for freedom: it will see freedom or die;
Yet does it give freedom value over death. Terez,
If any would drink of Liberty's well
He first must stoop at the pool of patience,
Not inactive, but lashed firm to wisdom's oars,
Riding the self-motioned swell of good sense.

TEREZ: Yet do I fear he will not attend our cause.

BIGTHANA:
Cast off such thoughts, they are death.
If freedom will not be mine, let me die.
Yet ere I fall these hands will do death
To royal neck.

TEREZ:
Ere your hands find their neck, my dagger
Would have found its mark.

BIGTHANA: But hush!
Ears unseen the conspiring air oft will breed.

Let's to the queen, and our awkward duty done,
Cast around our sights for one the king holds
In high esteem to advocate us our cause.

        [*Exeunt.*

Scene 4.—HAMAN'S *house. The living room.*

BILBO *surreptitiously helping himself to his master's wine. Enter* MIHESO.

MIHESO:
Bilbo, yet at the master's wine? This happy sport
Will tomorrow make wicked sport of you.

BILBO: Does Sikuru come?
A starry, starry evening ahead of him
Do I stand in my stoups and cups.
[*Enter* SIKURU.]
Sikuru! Sikuru! Though your very mouth
Were Susa's winepress, the vastest of Persia's vats,
You would not tonight match my cups.

SIKURU:
Miheso, take our wager. But hush!
[*He retraces his steps.*] I think I hear…
[*Peeping out*] …the master! Quick!
        [*Exit.*

[MIHESO *dashes out too, but* BILBO, *slowed by inebriation and the wine apparatus in his hands, seeks refuge under a table. Enter* HAMAN *and* ZERESH.]

HAMAN:
Had flattery not so thickened his sight,
He would have seen it was not I who lay
In prostrate state serene, but he himself,
Fabled king of Persia, jewelled monarch
Of the opulent East, emperor enthroned
Of the conquered world, by honey-drippings
Of sweet words felled, by slick of tongue slid.
Men grown in elevation and conceit fall quick
To flattery's tripping. From my square of floor
I heard the happy rumble of his stomach
Disporting in the juice of my words, and I saw
What always I had known: all power to topple
Is locked in a tongue's command. Today my tongue
Has made me prince; will not the selfsame tongue
Tomorrow raise me to power's pinnacle
Where by merest words I may about my shoulders
Gather me my dream? Nor can riches or fame
Or power, or other strong desire,
Outpeak this dream. But have my friends come?
Is my court a-fret for me? Bilbo! Bilbo!
Are they arrived? Bilbo! Bilbo! Bilbo!
[BILBO *crawls out, rear first.*]

BILBO: I go to your bidding, my master.

[*He creeps away amid the dumbfounded gaze of* HAMAN *and* ZERESH.]

HAMAN:
Has Vashti's madness swooped down here, even here?

ZERESH: And there was Vaizatha today…

HAMAN: That was wisdom, not madness.

ZERESH: Vaizatha is my baby!

HAMAN: Thirteen and fit to wield the sword!

ZERESH: Mad ways have lost me nine sons;
Should I watch this one, too, step to high parade
Of filial mischief?

HAMAN:
You should have borne me a girl-child. Inheriting
A sleek brain rich with cunning, a tongue
As may assure the gobbling turkey of comely beauty,
Such looks as would move the sun to jealous rage –
Sterling traits of her sapphire sire –
Would she not to the seat of Persia's Queen
Now be poised to sail with pinion ease?

ZERESH: Tradition yet would have barred her,
Not being daughter of the ranking brace of seven.

HAMAN:
Zeresh, this day did I humble tradition's back
And break the yoke of the Seven. I urged,
And the king listened; could he do otherwise?
He caught my counsel to wive in manner
Not by treaty or tradition forced,
Nor by pressure pressed, but in fancy's sweep
To take to breast a maiden sweet and fair,
Pliant, full pleasing, unstuck by nobility's
Stony core. And because he listened,
Bowing freely to my words, Susa's air
Tingles now with secret plans to swoop
Upon the sleeping realm and gather maidens
Of virgin breath and beauty.

ZERESH: A virgin swoop!

HAMAN:
Thus would the king in the lap of night,
Virgin sampling in private sport, find his queen.

ZERESH: O what a wailing will fill the land!

HAMAN:
A wailing sorry and sweet, yet not so sweet
As the wailing that will rent the land when I,
To the summits of influence ascended,
Let fall my dark and dread designs.

Act One

ZERESH: What designs, my lord?
[*Enter* BILBO.]

BILBO:
Master, your friends await your leisure.

HAMAN:
No more call me 'Master,' but 'Worthy Prince
   Haman,'
For thus did the king today himself call me;
Will you do less? [*Laughing*] How my friends will
   greet
This happy smile of fortune.
[*To* BILBO] Prepare me for court!

BILBO [*to Servants offstage*]: Miheso! Sikuru!
The master – er – Worthy Prince Haman stands for
   court!
[*Enter* MIHESO *and* SIKURU. *Together with* BILBO,
they groom HAMAN *extravagantly, waxing his
moustache, giving him a manicure, a pedicure,
changing robes, rings etc.*]

ZERESH: Haman, I asked: What designs?

HAMAN: Ah...
My secret of secrets. Harsh and dark! Dark and dread!
Only I know it; only I will know it –
Till the favouring season erupts it.

I have thrown bricks of hint to your ears,
And to your eyes have hurled a wedge of signs,
But hearing with dwarfish ears, and seeing
In glaze of cataract, you have known naught.

ZERESH: I begin to fear…

HAMAN:
Fear not, till the favouring season – then fear.

ZERESH:
This secret serpent you hold to your breast
Is rich, I think, with double-coursed venom.

HAMAN [*to grooming Servants*]: Enough!
[*The three Servants go to the door and assume the pose of guards.*]

ZERESH:
Though you design the world to blight and doom,
First fetch me back my baby.

HAMAN [*walking to the door*]:
Never more to Vaizatha ascribe that name!
Never ever! Hear me well: Never ever!
No name more unsaps a man than baby!

Act One

BILBO [*addressing* HAMAN'S *friends offstage*]:
                              The master –
Er – Worthy Prince Haman attends his court!

HAMAN [*half-out*]:
Zeresh, glitter yourself to a shining:
Your finest robe and finest gold! Let diamonds
On you sprout! Like the king, before my court
I'll summon my wife, but she'll not Vashti me;
No, Zeresh shall not, nor ever, Vashti me,
Else the wailing of Persia's seized virgins
Shall to her anguished screams be ditty soft.
[*His laughter, loud and chortling, fills the air.*]
                    [*Exits with Servants. Curtain.*

Act Two

Scene 1.—MORDECAI'S *house. Early morning.*

MORDECAI, ESTHER *and* NATHAN *astir.*

MORDECAI: Would you swear it so, Nathan?

NATHAN: Prudence bade me come with haste
Ere certainty cast a steady hand.

ESTHER:
Can a searching mind, Papa, not find ten reasons
Unmaliced that mix to keep her from home?

MORDECAI: Yet am I wary
Of this tale of virgin-gatherers.

ESTHER: Virgin-gatherers!
Can such stuff of fables be true today?

NATHAN:
Is Ahasuerus not king from end to end,
With power to spin and weave whim's utmost fancy?
If he's chosen this odd cut, who can say,

'Sire, stuff your design back into fable's bag
And clothe our frames only in the fabric
Of our trimmed and tailor-tapered judgment'?

MORDECAI:
If true, Rachael is doomed, for she is Jew.

NATHAN:
Concubinage knows not Persian, nor Jew,
Nor to shade of dark Ethiopian will curtsey,
But all alike in dungeon gloom inters.

MORDECAI:
The king's choice of queen could on Persian tresses fall,
Or on the sheen of sable Afric sit,
But never could it on Jewish brow alight.
If Rachael were but what she is, I would say,
'Maid! Hope yet, for yet you may be queen.'
But Rachael is Jew, oiled through with Hebrew blood.
[*Pause.*]
And yet –

ESTHER: And yet?

MORDECAI:
If she were to seal her lips to race and kin
Who could say to her, 'Hold! I smell you Jew!'?

NATHAN:
We plunge deep when we first should skim the top.
Now that I have rallied you to watchfulness
I may with freer stride go to probe the mist.

MORDECAI:
And I, earlier than my wont, shall span the gate:
The night-post should know the stirrings of the night.

NATHAN:
Esther, take not lightly our cautions…
[*Pause.*]
Mordecai…

MORDECAI: Friend…

NATHAN:
Now is reason robust to wring that matter out –
Though we wring Esther through with tears.
[*He leaves. Silence.*]

ESTHER: Rachael – I knew the girl…

MORDECAI: Let it not be true…

ESTHER:
She had a face the very picture of grace –

Act Two

MORDECAI: She is Jew!
O wisdom, give her a deep and prudent mind!
Seal her lips to race and kin, and let not Jew
Escape her lips, or eye pry her deep to knowing!
[*Pause.*]
Esther, I must to the gate: I cannot wait
To know if this spectre walks with living blood,
For then we must look more closely to you.

ESTHER: You know me, Papa.

MORDECAI: I shall not loosely unmoor my hope.

ESTHER: If it be covert malaise…

MORDECAI: No, 'tis no ailment.

ESTHER: Then let me be.
Not all will marry who are maids.

MORDECAI:
I fear I coddle you to our mutual harm,
But the hour begs other concerns; I must go.
[*He goes to the door.*]
O that it should be the fleshless echo
Of a dream, unsubstanced and vanishing!

ESTHER:
It is. I fear not you'll return to say
All is well, as my heart presages me.

MORDECAI:
Yes, but hold caution dearly to your breast,
Nor venturing out, nor dropping within your guard.

ESTHER: I will heed you well, my father.
[*Exit* MORDECAI.
[ESTHER *commences housework. Suddenly* MORDECAI *returns.*]

MORDECAI: Daughter, bar the door.

ESTHER: Papa!
Will they storm closed doors to sack house and lodge?

MORDECAI:
I care not to fill Snare's nest with ready hatch
Or glad the prowler with easy catch.
Slip the bar, my child.

ESTHER:
Why worry, Papa? Can palace splendour
Ever woo from me name of race and kin?

MORDECAI: Esther!

Act Two

ESTHER: I but jest, Papa.
[MORDECAI *stares disconcertingly at her.*]

MORDECAI: Sick jokes make poor jest.
[*Pause. He leaves.*]

ESTHER [*shaking her head*]: Papa...
[*She bars the door and continues with her chores. Suddenly the door is tried, and when found barred, there is a knocking. ESTHER, amused, refrains awhile from opening the door.*]

MORDECAI [*outside the door*]: Esther... Esther...

ESTHER: Papa...
[*She opens the door. MORDECAI enters and in a gesture of anxious affection, proceeds to hug his daughter. Then he sets off again.*]

MORDECAI [*going*]:
Tread softly, child... Softly...
                    [*Exit.*
[ESTHER, *bemused at her father's anxiety, recommences chores. After a while the door is tried again and there is a knocking as before.*]

ESTHER [*going to the door*]: Oh Papa...
[*She opens the door. Soldiers. She freezes, then screams, tries to shut the door, but they burst in and*

chase her, and soon seize her, screaming and scratching and struggling.]
[*Being dragged off*] No! No! No! No-o-o-o!
[*Exeunt.*
[*On stage nothing but debris, receding screams, and a dying light.*]

Scene 2.—*A secluded place in the palace.*

Enter BIGTHANA *and* TEREZ.

BIGTHANA:
And no more able advocate is there
Than this courtier. Here is the place; we wait here.
[*They wait.*]
He has so swiftly won the king's love,
And may by the current of this love
Steer the king's face to sights beneath his gaze
And to our favour prompt royal nod.

TEREZ:
Bigthana, it would serve us well, I think,
To throw ourselves with bowed knees before the king
And ourselves lay our suit at royal feet.

BIGTHANA:
And I, Terez, do think your quivering pulse
Will bring us yet to fine and wondrous harm.
The scrub-a-dub slave knows 'tis who woos protocol

Quickly finds his way to royal grace. Besides,
The king's eyes brim to froth with wiving,
And only one sunk in his favoured love
May catch his gaze and anchor him to our suit.

TEREZ:
Should we not then wait till his wiving is done
And to the new queen give our suit?

BIGTHANA:
Would you to woman's whim assign your life?
Unschooled by Vashti then you stand, untrained
In simplest prudence.

TEREZ:
This man you speak of – has he heart enough
To hold our trust?
[*Enter* HAMAN.]

BIGTHANA: Hush! 'Tis he.

HAMAN:
Bigthana, is that you I spy, worthy master
Of the king's guard? And this – this must be him
You would have me calm.

BIGTHANA: Lord Haman!

[*Introducing* TEREZ]
Terez, my deputy, my friend; colleaguèd
As one with me in this matter of the suit.

HAMAN: Terez,
Do you neither know me nor have heard of me
That you would not clap and say, 'Ah, 'tis done;
Now Haman has our suit freedom comes to roost'?
Need I say aught, or speak, or speaking, speak much?
Let all speaking henceforth be before the king
Who, as I pause to stand with you, awaits
My chin of fellowship; whom, for the love
Of you who trust me, I shall with sturdy words
Prod to justice; for right flanks you left and right,
Your suit is just and fair. And though justice
May be slow to birth or slack to rise,
Who better than I who hold the king's ear,
To pull it or tug it, or strike it
Or lash it, or whip it, or failing thus,
Gently to lead it to court with garland
Of flattery or scent of bulging purse, and there
Let it take its course? Need I speak much?
But hold yourselves strong to your trust in me,
While I to the king will go, my friends,
And hold him to your just and worthy cause.
[*He starts off.*]
Terez, do your fears not now subside?
Nor cry with Bigthana to know why
I so freely would do this thing for you,

Else cry to know why the wind so blusterily blows,
Or why the tree so silently grows,
Or why the mind, with baseless fears infested,
Knows not what it knows. I go, my friends,
I go.
  [*Exit.*

BIGTHANA [*watching him go*]:
As I have faithfully guarded the king,
So, noble Haman, may your faithfulness
Be your guard. [*To* TEREZ] Do you not now see?

TEREZ:
I do not like his eyes; they are like flares
That snare men at night to their doom.

BIGTHANA:
Let his eyes haunt their orbs, his tongue
Is all we need.

TEREZ:
I neither care for his tongue; it slides too smooth
In its groove.

BIGTHANA:
The better to slide the king to our favour.
But come, Terez, nor whinge my life to death
With womanish fears! Come!

[*He leaves, but* TEREZ *remains pondering. Lights fade.*]

Scene 3.—MORDECAI'S *house. The living room.*

MORDECAI, *crushed by dejection. He sits. He stands. He paces. He sits. His hands strap his head. A knock on the door. Ignored. The knock again, loud. Ignored. The knocking becomes persistent.*

NATHAN [*outside the door*]:
Mordecai! ... Mordecai! ... Mordecai!

MORDECAI [*quietly to himself, remaining seated*]:
Nathan...

NATHAN [*still knocking*]: Mordecai!

MORDECAI [*musingly*]: Nathan...
[*During a lull in the knocking he abstractedly rises to open the door.*]
[*Seeing* NATHAN]
The myrtle of life from here is gone;
And nothing blooms now but decay and death's
    orchid.
[*He walks off abruptly to his seat.* NATHAN *enters. Awkward silence.*]

NATHAN: When I heard... Oh Mordecai...
[*He starts towards* MORDECAI.]

MORDECAI [*rebuffing him*]: No! No!
[*Pause.*]
[*Abstractedly*] They took her. My Esther is gone,
My Hadassah, my myrtle blossom…
[*Silence.* NATHAN *sits.*]
Myself has done this deed. 'Find your maid her man,'
Said all, but had Mordecai ears to hear?
Filled to deafness were my ears by the beat
That holds me thralled, binds me from the homeland,
And now has bound my daughter to the court
Of cruel concubinage. Alas! Woe is me!
Oh, alas!

NATHAN: Be a man.

MORDECAI:
Alas that I'm a man and no unfeeling beast!
Else who is a man? Lay here bronze for flesh
And I shall be that man of silent lips;
Or lend me sodden sense of brutish beast
And I shall be him you would have me be;
Or give me marble shard and take this heart –
But no heart grows here now: it fell – alas! –
When my myrtle blossom did fall. I am a man.
But what a man I am, who, with slaughterous hand
Of omission, has slain his very own!

NATHAN: She is not dead.

MORDECAI:
She is. And worse than dead who no more
May freedom's air kiss, or love's breath feel,
Or ever the wonders of wedlock know.
And who can say, who knows, Nathan, who knows
What other spectre, for this label of Jew,
Now combines with several deaths to seal her fate.

NATHAN:
Plague not your mind with conjured terrors.

MORDECAI:
But she will not be signalled Jew
Or named by race or kin; I know it, Nathan,
I know it! Was it not she who said:
'Why worry, Papa? Can palace splendour
Ever woo from me name of race and kin?'
Though said in ill-jest, it rings now with peal
Of sober vow. Nathan, do you not think,
Do you not think, Nathan, it is as I say?
'Why worry, Papa?' she said. 'Why worry?
Can palace splendour…' 'Can palace splendour
Ever woo from me name of race and kin?'
'Can palace splendour…' Nathan, her very phrase
Brains me through with iron peals. Naught will
    squeeze
Jew's name from her or link her blood to mine.
Esther! Hide well your Jewry and live!
Live, my daughter! Mordecai twice will stand –

Once for you and once for him –
With twin strips of Jew banding his brow
To double dare the sniggering world!

NATHAN:
These walls pump your thoughts to battering frenzy.

MORDECAI: Wretched man that I am!

NATHAN:
Come away, Mordecai, and let the open air
From dread lift your thoughts; let's escape these walls.

MORDECAI: Fall on me, walls!

NATHAN: Come!

MORDECAI: No!
[*Pause.*]

NATHAN: Mordecai…
[*Pause.*]

MORDECAI:
Would you venture the Garden of Spice,
The restful grove by the Cinnamon Gate?

NATHAN: The palace?

MORDECAI:
Where soft breezes by the harem's east quarters

Dandle scents – there is the place to be:
Harem whisperings flutter the wind there;
I could hear news of my myrtle blossom…

NATHAN:
Then what holds us here? Let's yonder heel our way!
[Exeunt.

Scene 4.—HAMAN'S *house. The living room.*

Enter HAMAN *and* ZERESH.

HAMAN:
I disavow all that bring no gain;
You know me well, Zeresh.

ZERESH:
Is it no gain to win me a son?

HAMAN:
I've seeded you ten sons. Ten!
Had I sniffed my life along the path
Of barren emotions as you would have me do,
I would not now reek princely air and power.
I've raised myself to grand and lofty heights
By fixing my sights ever on gain.
Who love not profit sit reach in folly;
Who live not for gain come soon to pain –
As Bigthana and Terez soon will know.

[*Laughs*] Call them not 'Bigthana' and 'Terez'
But 'Folly' and 'Folly.' Had they reasoned
And asked but this: 'What gain for Haman,
Why expect Haman to hold our cause?'
Then would they not have spent garlic breath
To conscript me ally and advocate.
But let them wait and wait and sit in folly –
Haman goes nowhere for them.

ZERESH:

What have I to do with Bigthana and Terez,
Two fatted eunuch-calves? We speak of Haman's son.

HAMAN:

Ha! Two fatted eunuch-calves… I like well
The ring of your tag and will twist it
To play and confound their folly. Ha!

ZERESH:

The stones prate with blood
Where Vaizatha is set to walk…

HAMAN:

Zeresh, grill not yourself to fever,
Nor grudge the lad his rein, but set yourself
To stony calm, and your sights to gain.

ZERESH:

He's my son, I'm his mother;

But that a mother's want be satisfied,
What more gain need I protest?
[HAMAN *shrugs disdainfully.*]
He baits them; like his brothers, he baits them.
Haman, I fear that soon, like his brothers
Who from home and rein have strayed away,
Jewish blood, from guiltless vein, will gout his thumb.

HAMAN:
Then would he be the man I desire of him.
[*His laughter rouses the air as lights fade.*]

   Scene 5.—*The King's palace. His bed-chamber.*

HEGAI *before the King.*

KING AHASUERUS: Hegai…

HEGAI [*prostrating*]: My king.

KING AHASUERUS:
Dogs have their bitches, peasants their wenches,
Bond slaves their slattern maids, but your king,
Your king can find his sail nor lift nor wind.

HEGAI:
My king, the wind tonight shall swell the seas.

KING AHASUERUS:
The seas swell and swarm with legs and arms

And nectared breasts, the scented tokens
Of your happy labours; but where, harem chief,
Is the dew, the cleansing breath I seek?

HEGAI:
My efforts, O king, now have filled the catching net.

KING AHASUERUS:
Your efforts have left my mind unmated,
My heart unfulfilled. These scented maids
That nightly swamp my sight with virgin wares
Spark in me no burning fire, quench no thirst.
I need more than honey, much more lasting fare.

HEGAI:
She stands now at the door,
She whom the king has waited for.

KING AHASUERUS:
You know not the king's heart.

HEGAI: As the king lives –

KING AHASUERUS: Patience has fled my breast!

HEGAI:
She stands at the door, O king;
Had her fire not so fiercely raged,
I had brought her sooner to the king.

KING AHASUERUS:
Do you know the leap of my desire,
Know my pith and deepest want?

HEGAI:
I know only, my king,
That out there stands she who would be queen.
[*Pause.*]

KING AHASUERUS:
Let me see this wonder, Hegai;
This object of your so strong confidence.

HEGAI: As the king desires.
[*He goes to the door.*]
[*Calling*] The king awaits the virgin Esther!
[*Enter* ESTHER. *She is framed by the guards* HATHACH *and* MANSUR, *who bow and leave.* ESTHER *stands, her grace supreme, her beauty ethereal. The King is some paces away, his back turned to her.* HEGAI *pauses, watches. Then a smile lights up his face, and he gently departs, shutting the door and leaving* ESTHER *alone with the King.* ESTHER *waits. The King remains in pose, face averted from her. Eventually he turns. Their eyes lock. For one interminable moment. Lights dim. Curtain.*]

Act Three

Scene 1.—*Palace grounds. The Garden of Spice, adjoining the harem.*

MORDECAI *is snooping for news on* ESTHER. *Hearing women's laughter, he slips behind some shrubs but re-emerges when no one appears. But he soon returns to cover when he hears the sound of approach along one of the numerous paths that serve the garden. Enter* NATHAN.

NATHAN [*in muted call*]: Mordecai! … Mordecai!

MORDECAI [*emerging*]:
Nathan! What strange thing brings you here?

NATHAN: One last farewell, friend.

MORDECAI: Did any say I was here?

NATHAN:
None needed to say what already I knew:
Not at your post, nor at home, only could mean
The Garden of Spice, foraging the air
For whispers on Esther.

[*Voices are heard.* MORDECAI *prepares to dive for cover, but the voices fade.*]

NATHAN:
Mordecai, this squirrel-crabbing
Unbecomes the father of Persia's queen.

MORDECAI:
Was it for this you came? To prate me?

NATHAN:
Will men not laugh to see the queen's father
In pose of hunting crab? – Legs ascrabble,
Hands in mantis curve, ears swivelling the air,
Neck craned aloft to gobble the whispering wind?
Esther! Queen of Persia! Hie thee hither
To see your father!

MORDECAI:
Hush! None in palace circle names me her father;
And let lie the knowledge in iron secrecy.

NATHAN: Mordecai, hold back no more.

MORDECAI: Ah, 'twas for this you came!

NATHAN:
'Tis not too late to unhoist this porterage
Of obduracy and come with me;
The caravans will wait.

MORDECAI:

Your needling words all of last night left me
 unmarked,
Though they whined screeching high and droned
 snoring low;
Think now to sink in a barb?

NATHAN:

The soil of your father's fathers, Mordecai,
Fain would see the labour of your arm.

MORDECAI: I labour here, and here remain.

NATHAN:

Tending alien fields with an arm that forsakes
The very head and fount of his strength?

MORDECAI:

My daughter is here, and here lies my fate.

NATHAN:

Your daughter no more, but Persia's maid.
The realm, to gain a queen, has disfathered you.
Can you not see? Your very word to Esther
Has joined in fatal lock with the time's mischief
To bar her ever from you, and you from her.
What sense and logic then straddle your choice to stay?

MORDECAI:
Sense and logic are but fallible servants of the mind
And must in season yield to impulse deep sprung;
But peer with me with eyes that glean the past
And tell me if I dissemble to say:
Logic unseen today, time does in time display.

NATHAN:
Unvalued Porter to Persia! When in your land
Your qualities could spin you golden robes!
You bend here in second-class stoop when at home
Your faculties, bright to the discerning eye,
Could sweep you on to golden station.
Mordecai, why beat this path of foolishness?

MORDECAI:
The light within that lights my path –

NATHAN:
And sends you a-crabbing and squirrelling in turns?
That light is false!

MORDECAI:
Then spare the homeland a deceiving light.
But no more – I hear voices…

NATHAN: Let men rename you Stubborn!

MORDECAI: Quick, Nathan!

Act Three

NATHAN [*going off*]:
Bear alone the fool's fardel on your pate!

MORDECAI [*slipping behind shrubs*]:
Hide, Nathan – hide!

NATHAN: When you wake to sense
Come scour for me in our fathers' pastures.
                                        [*Exit.*
[MORDECAI *under cover. Enter* HAMAN *with*
BIGTHANA *and* TEREZ.]

HAMAN:
But he would not hear of it, and as I pleaded,
His rage grew. At length he drove me off:
'Hence!' he roared. 'And if again you furnish suit
Of those slaves, those fatted eunuch-calves,
Your head with theirs, in roll of death, will race!'
I tried my best, my friends, I tried my best –
To the beck and edge of my honest neck.
[*Pause.*]
But grieve not, nor cast to watery depths your hope;
Joy yet with the sun may rise to startle sorrow.
[*Pause.*]
Ah well, I must leave you now, my friends,
To rest at home this still trembling frame
Far from regal roar. Farewell, friends; farewell!
                                        [*Exit.*

TEREZ [*hurling his cloak to the ground in rage*]:
Tonight the king dies!

BIGTHANA: Hush!
[*He beckons* TEREZ *away from* HAMAN'S *trail. They move and stop close to* MORDECAI'S *hiding place.*]
I'm chief of the king's guard,
His very life oystered in my hands,
Yet to him I'm no man…

TEREZ: He dies tonight!

BIGTHANA:
…But a slave to be ranked below the rack-ribbed cur,
And with him to bear the boot of scorn,
Whimpering target for the speeding phlegm.
Yes, Terez, this very night the king shall die,
But not by dagger or mauling hands
Lest suspicion drifts our way.

TEREZ:
What care I for suspicion? My life is done.

BIGTHANA:
If we can administer death and live, why die?

TEREZ: My keen blade it is will find his heart.

BIGTHANA: No!
No king's death for him, nor royal snuffing out,
But death by pauses in cruellest venom.

Act Three

TEREZ: Poison?

BIGTHANA:
Sting of scorpion with spit of silver asp –
I have the thing. Brewed tasteless in sapsute herb,
Who can tell, when we his night cup have conjoined,
That this or that man did it? Terez, were fear
Encamped with me, I would fear the screams
That would rive the night and stop the heart
Of his new-found queen.

TEREZ:
That they slight the cries of a hapless slave
Fresh thrust into eunuchry, is all I ask.

BIGTHANA:
Come! The hour summons us now to careful steps
In the night's dark and poison-deep emprise.
                              [*Exeunt.*
[MORDECAI *emerges. He heads for an exit. A sound. He turns. It is* TEREZ, *returned for the cloak he hurled to the ground. Their eyes lock. A stillness.* MORDECAI *hastens away.* TEREZ, *rooted to the spot, gazes after him. Lights fade.*]

Scene 2.—*The King's palace. A lounge.*

The King lounging, waited upon by Servants and Attendants.

KING AHASUERUS: Loose the wine!

[*A Servant fills his cup. Enter* ESTHER.]
No more! Take this cup from me!
My queen is fountain fresh enough to cool my thirst.
No more tonight of wine, but my bedside cup.
Esther, see how quickly you reform me.

ESTHER: I'll know it, my lord,
When your night cup is drained of frequency.

KING AHASUERUS: That will be the death of me;
But who knows how Esther yet may ransom me.

ESTHER [*to Attendants*]: I'll serve the king.
Let all go now. Go now, everyone.
[*Servants and Attendants leave.*]
[ESTHER, *during the following, occasionally offers the King fruits, sweetmeats etc.*]

KING AHASUERUS:
Your hair… it fell just so that fragrant night…

ESTHER:
Does your heart, like mine, swoon in memory's sway?

KING AHASUERUS:
I'm king: I swoon not. Yet do I remember,
As though 'twere my very own painting,
The flush and every hue of that gentle night.
[*Pause.*]
Esther,
Would you truly have done the thing you said?

Act Three

ESTHER: 'Twas all that kept my wits to me –
[*She unsheathes the dagger at the King's waist.*]
– And soft to Hegai's labours.
All I asked, as I sank it deep to me,
Was to see rage storm your shock-ridden eyes
As at your feet your craving fell unfed.

KING AHASUERUS [*retrieving the dagger*]:
Not yours, but my heart, would have held the blade;
For so swiftly did my heart, at sight of you,
Flee this breast to live in yours, my Esther.
And you did still pierce it: I never see you
But your beauty wounds me through.

ESTHER:
'Twas your eyes, piercing the veil of gloom
That strange and wondrous night, that tranced me
To new perceiving: here stood my life,
And little had known it; here, the very end
Of all my waiting; the reason at last
For nuptial dilatoriness, my daffodil mind,
Those tears that ever fell to ambush all wedlock talk.
Drop all daggers, then said I, and walk the shine
Of love's own glint.

KING AHASUERUS [*taking her hand to his lips*]:
My very heart and queen…

ESTHER: That reputation
Ever did spin such fearful cape around you…

KING AHASUERUS:
You know me not sifting through, my Esther.
But let me ever hide wrathful face from you.
When I vent deadly fume, as oft to men's peril
I have done, lock me firm sanctum walls!
Yet, Esther, perchance you've cured me my ailment,
Though I cannot, it seems, cure you your mystery.

ESTHER: What mystery, my lord?

KING AHASUERUS:
None is born but into kin and lineage.
There's much I fain would unkernel you of.

ESTHER:
Orphans, if they will live, must escape the past:
'Tis no more than that, my king. I was cleft,
Sprung of parents perished, an only child.

KING AHASUERUS:
Had I one to spare me administration's
Tiresome knotting – a chief minister, say –
I would, untugged by swerving imperial thoughts,
With searching mind voyage the past with you.

ESTHER: The waters I fain would chart
But beckon ahead in oceans unsailed.

KING AHASUERUS:
He's pleased me much, this Haman.

ESTHER: Haman?

KING AHASUERUS:
His shoulders, sturdy in the thickets of counsel,
And in administration of much robust hew,
Better than Memucan or one of the Seven
May the heavy palm of chief minister bear.

ESTHER: Haman as chief minister?

KING AHASUERUS: Do you not see?

ESTHER: Surely not Haman!

KING AHASUERUS:
Ah, but you're slight of frame in matters of state.

ESTHER: Not so slight as my lord thinks.
[*A bang at the portals.*]

KING AHASUERUS: Come!
[*Enter* HARBONA.]

HARBONA: My lord, a letter for the queen.

KING AHASUERUS [*taking it*]:
A letter for the queen?

[*Waves* HARBONA *off and passes the letter to* ESTHER.]
Who, unknown to me, has known the curve of your branch?

ESTHER: But none, my lord!
[*She reads the letter, then hastily passes it back to the King.*]
Read, my lord!
[*The King takes it.*]

KING AHASUERUS:
'Tis signed by one called Mordecai…
[*He reads it through silently, then returns to the core.*]
…And tonight plan to lace his bedside wine…
[*He stares at* ESTHER.]
Bigthana and Terez? … Bigthana? … Terez?
Can this be true?

ESTHER:
Were it not true, Mordecai would not –

KING AHASUERUS: Mordecai…

ESTHER: 'Tis true, my lord, 'tis true!
[*Pause.*]
Act swiftly, my lord.

KING AHASUERUS: Yes…

Act Three

ESTHER:
But discreetly, ranging yourself with the shield
Of suspicion: perchance the two act not alone…

KING AHASUERUS:
Words weighed to breaking with golden sense;
Therefore must I find me clever help
To rake the matter through: one I trust
To the very falter of closing breath…
[*Pause.*] Haman…

ESTHER: Not Haman, my lord!
[*The King sounds gong for Attendant. Enter* HARBONA.]

KING AHASUERUS:
Hold your life only to race Haman here! Go!
[*Exit* HARBONA.]
                                  None moves swifter
Or more surely about my business than Haman.

ESTHER: Not Haman…

KING AHASUERUS [*facing her*]:
And why not Haman?
[*Silence. Lights fade.*]

    Scene 3.—*A secluded place in the palace.*

BIGTHANA *and* TEREZ *in altercation.*

BIGTHANA: Your fretting wears me to anger.

TEREZ: We must set on his trail!

BIGTHANA: 'Tis a foolish hunter
Who targets jackals on the lion's trail.

TEREZ: Jackals
In fleeing oft signal lions to alarm.

BIGTHANA:
Why then did you not halt his fleeing?

TEREZ:
I tire of words! We must stop him
Ere he tolls vigilance to warding stance
And bays the world to us!
[*Enter* HAMAN.]

HAMAN:
Bigthana, ho! Good news! Good news! Rejoice!
'Tis wondrous news! Once more for you, my friends,
Have I braved the crush of the lion's jaws!
And to what returns! What rich recompense!
Despondent that my friends were despondent,
In pain from the pain of those who sought me
And left unfed, I chafed and knew no rest,
But chiselled my brain to a flaming edge,
Till brilliance furnished me new device
To test the depth of the king's reserve;
And so with tongue bright and sharp with new plea,

Act Three

And words adrip and quivering with new charm,
I stood before the king – so stood I before him –
[*In the ensuing,* HAMAN *is engaged in manoeuvring the two officers to positions backing the exit.*]
No, 'twas not so – here was the king, and I here…
No, no, the king was here – stand thus, this way…
Was the king here? No, he was here, here –
Oh, 'tis wondrous news – I was here, the king there…
Ah, but the king was sitting – sit, sit, do sit…
Yes, the king sat, and I bowed before the king
As all must bow. I bowed. Watch as I did bow,
For the cue is in the bowing, a sign –
Ah, Bigthana, this day are you set free –
Terez! O Terez! Watch now, watch me now!
I did fold and bow in manner piteous…
Thus did I bow, thus…
[*As he engages in an elaborate display of mock obeisance, Guards slip in from behind and bludgeon* BIGTHANA *and* TEREZ, *trussing them up.*]
[*Rising and gloating*]   Ha!
Brawn, though great, to mightier brain must fall.
Good news! Good news! Indeed are you tonight
From the gelding bonds of life truly freed.
If that be not good news, pray, what then is?
[*His laughter fills the air as the Guards cart off the two. Lights fade.*]

Scene 4.—*The King's palace. The lounge as before.*

ESTHER *and the King alone.*

KING AHASUERUS:
It is not that which harrows me!

ESTHER: What then is it, my lord?
[*A bang at the portals.*]

KING AHASUERUS: Enter!
[*Enter* HARBONA.]

HARBONA:
Lord Haman, O king, sends news of the slaves' arrest,
And will himself, when all enquiry is done,
Be forthwith here.

KING AHASUERUS:
The man is unfellowed, in loyalty matchless.
                    [*Exit* HARBONA.
[*To* ESTHER] And you said, 'Not Haman, my lord!' –
Behold the withering of feeble judgment!
Man! Henceforth despair of woman's counsel!
Beware, too, her soft beguiling fragrance!

ESTHER: I spoke but caution, my king.

KING AHASUERUS: Who is Mordecai?

ESTHER: Mordecai, my lord?

Act Three

KING AHASUERUS: Mordecai!

ESTHER:
Does not my lord know him, who governs his gate?

KING AHASUERUS:
Should rabble sit encrystalled in the king's eye?
[*Pause.*]
'Twas my life conspiracy whispered for,
But warning meanders queenward. Why so?
[*Pause.*]
Why?

ESTHER:
Many are the reasons, my lord, that may account –

KING AHASUERUS:
Save all and give but one! One!

ESTHER:
Might not he have deemed it wiser?

KING AHASUERUS [*tossing the letter away*]:
I did therein perceive a coddling tone…

ESTHER:
And I that danger rose to strike one man
And courage in another rose to foil it.

KING AHASUERUS: You shuffle with me.

ESTHER: I fear for your life, my lord.

KING AHASUERUS: Fear for yours!
[*A bang at the portals.*]
Enter!
[*Enter* HAMAN.]

HAMAN: Live for ever, O king! Live for ever!

KING AHASUERUS:
How your timing glistens with perfection!

HAMAN:
Speedy and prompt in my fashion, my lord.

KING AHASUERUS:
It is well there is one on whose shoulders
Reliance will not squirm to rest. What report?

HAMAN:
None else was party to the scheme of the two.
Their plot was hatched the day that Vashti fell.

KING AHASUERUS:
How is it queens and the raw rabble
Have walked together and played the cosy?

HAMAN:
Vashti, for sundry services performed
In petty palace concerns, did sometime

Act Three

Make the two a promise of manumission
Which when the queen fell they feared had lapsed.

KING AHASUERUS:
Fools! It was theirs for the asking.

HAMAN:
Fools indeed, my lord; fools! Peerless fools!
Hatching in their folly the wickedness
That in time would grow to smother them.
This very night, by poisoned goblet,
In pain and cruellest agony, the king's life –
Forbid it! – to their mocking eyes – forbid it!
Oh, forbid it! Forbid it! Forbid it!

KING AHASUERUS:
Un-neck the slaves! Off with their heads!

HAMAN:
Their heads have jumped the hacking-saw, my lord,
And rest now in gory trays tranquil.

KING AHASUERUS [*to* ESTHER]:
Do you not see? Do you not hear?
Ere the thought lifts the tongue the deed is done.
Haman, walk not out this chamber on earthen feet,
But go forth on silver stilts my chief minister –
Above all Persia's noble princes raised,
And to none ranking second but the king himself.

HAMAN: Chief minister… Chief minister?
[*Chuckles.*]

KING AHASUERUS:
This pleasure that swells and swamps your eyes
Is of breed that pleases me. And of nature,
I little doubt, pleasing to the queen.
Esther…

ESTHER: My lord?

KING AHASUERUS:
Do I lie? Does it not please you?
[*Pause.*]

ESTHER:
When evil bows to justice only evil grieves.

HAMAN:
Will this not lead the keen and wise in heart
To bow the knee to me? Chief minister…

KING AHASUERUS:
Would you have men bow to you?

HAMAN:
Forbid the king to think me vain…

KING AHASUERUS:
It is yours. Let men bow as you desire;

Set the scribes to scroll and vent the order.
Go now to this first task in highest office.

HAMAN:
I go, my king, with blinding joy!
Live for ever, great King Ahasuerus!
Emperor of the ranging earth, live for ever!
Live for ever, great king! O live for ever!
                                        [*Exit.*

KING AHASUERUS: Your answer, Esther.

ESTHER: My lord?

KING AHASUERUS: Answer!
[*Silence.*]
You bleed my patience.
[*Pause.*]
Esther…
[*Pause.*]
Esther!

ESTHER [*terrified at his vehemence*]:
Is… Is this you, my lord?

KING AHASUERUS: Mordecai – what is he to you?

ESTHER: Is this the king…?

KING AHASUERUS: Mordecai!

ESTHER: My lord…

KING AHASUERUS: Speak!

ESTHER [*falling at his feet*]: My king…

KING AHASUERUS: King?
A king defied is a king in slime enthroned.
Speak therefore!
[*Silence.*]
Speak, I say! Speak!
[*He thrusts her violently away.*]
What guilt clamps your lips?
What secret sin forbids your tongue the shape of speech?
[*Storming at her*] Out with it!
[*He grabs and shakes her fiercely.*]

ESTHER: Spare me, my lord!

KING AHASUERUS: Disgorge it!

ESTHER: Spare me!

KING AHASUERUS: Now!

ESTHER: Oh!

KING AHASUERUS: Now, I say!

ESTHER: I beg of you!

Act Three

KING AHASUERUS: Now!

ESTHER: Oh! Oh! Oh!
[*She manages to escape from the lounge. The King seethes and then slams his fists around, sending whatever is in his way crashing. Lights fade.*]

Scene 5.—*The palace gate. Busy atmosphere.*

MORDECAI *at his booth near the palace entrance. Suitors and others in little groups chatter away. Enter* AMOS. *He goes to* MORDECAI *to complete formalities necessary for palace admission.*

MORDECAI: Amos! What business today?

AMOS: Still nothing, Mordecai?

MORDECAI: What business, Amos?

AMOS: The stables. Still nothing?

MORDECAI:
Play not that string with breaking motion.

AMOS:
I stand not alone; all of Susa wonders:
Mordecai's word saves the king and gifts to men
Freely flow, but none to Mordecai. Why?

MORDECAI:
I hanker not for the piffle of man's reward.

AMOS:
He shunned by king for bounty famed is Jew;
And he over-laurelled with prize, Jew hater.
Is this not cause enough to rouse an iron brow?

MORDECAI:
The sun shall rise though every dog should bark.

AMOS: And as blast in cloudy overcast,
These bowing bells that manic the very blood!

MORDECAI [*amused*]:
I bear that no more than curious oddity:
What abnormality has gone and sired.
[*Suddenly from offstage come bell-chimes and peals of 'The chief minister! The chief minister!'*]

AMOS [*laughing*]:
My pass! Quick! I wish no acquaintanceship
With abnormality's new-fledged offspring!
[MORDECAI, *laughing, hands him his pass and* AMOS *disappears into the palace. Enter* HAMAN. *He is preceded by* 1st BOY *who rings bell-chimes, and followed by* 2nd BOY *who holds the train of his extensive robe and cries* 'The chief minister! The chief minister!' *at which each group of Suitors and persons approached bows in homage,* MORDECAI *alone staying unbowed. At the entrance arch, the Guards, with deep bows, admit* HAMAN, *but before he disappears into the palace* 2nd BOY, *having watched* MORDECAI *markedly, stops* HAMAN.]

2nd BOY:
My lord Haman, I note full well today
The porter lugs a careless head unbowed.
[HAMAN, *stunned, retraces his steps to* MORDECAI. *Chimes are rung and peals cried, causing all to bow except* MORDECAI, *who remains seated in rigid nonchalance.*]

HAMAN: Is it insanity's mischief
That compels you howl ignorance
Of royal order, the king's command?
[MORDECAI *remains nonchalant.*]
Is this thing possessed of living powers?
[MORDECAI *gives them his back.*]
[*To* 1st BOY]
Ask the slave! Ask him why he will not bow!

1st BOY:
Lord Haman, chief minister of Persia's empire,
Asks, porter at the king's gate, why you will not bow.
[*Long pause.*]

MORDECAI: I am a Jew.

1st BOY [*to* HAMAN]: He says he's a Jew.

HAMAN: Silence! Have I not ears?
[*Silence.* HAMAN *glares at* MORDECAI, *but* MORDECAI *is looking away. At length* MORDECAI *turns to return* HAMAN'S *gaze. The two glare at each other.*]

HAMAN: A Jew!
[*Pause.*]
A Jew without a beard.
[*Pause.*]
A beardless Jew. [*Pause.*] A Jew!
[*Pause.*]
[*To onlookers*] Your Jew fears not death…
[*Pause.*]
Yet is there a scourge that may besiege a man
Worse by far than death or the fear of death.
[*Pause.*]
Jew!
[*Pause.*]
My scourge on you, Jew, face-deep in agony
Will bend you yet to gulp and chew this dust!
Chew well your rage of victory now! Chew it!
For you shall chew and choke on dirt, when I,
Before the selfsame eyes that watch you now
And all of Susa viewing, shall on you slam
My wedge of rage and scourge you to the grave!
Else call me not Haman! Call me not Haman
Son of Hammedatha, with venom blood
Of Agagite flowing! [*To his boys*] Come!
　　　[*Exeunt* HAMAN *and his train. Lights fade.*]

Scene 6.—*The King's lounge.*

The King in a state of expectancy. Servants attending. Enter an Attendant.

Act Three

ATTENDANT: The Queen Esther!
[*Enter* ESTHER *flanked by* HATHACH *and* MANSUR. *She takes a few steps and then stands apprehensively. The King stares at her a long moment.*]

KING AHASUERUS [*to Attendants*]: Go!
[*All depart, leaving only the King and* ESTHER.]
Doubt not, Esther, that I love you.

ESTHER: My lord…
[*Her attempt to move to the King is stopped brusquely by him.*]

KING AHASUERUS: Therefore have I summoned
    you.
[*Pause.*]
I could have you and the man Mordecai racked
Till your joint screams divulged your joint secrets,
But love enfeebles me and slows the hand of wrath;
Yet 'tis none but the selfsame love which now,
With jealous knife, scrapes my burning brow
Of reason, and skins me deep to frenzy:
I trust no moment's calm; it but masks vicious spark.
Therefore speak; tell me all there is to know,
Leave nothing out.
[*Silence.*]
                          Esther,
When I, despairing of women and of love,
Sat my face deep in slime, yours was the breath

That lifted me to purity again.
Was your lifting only to perfect your dumping?

ESTHER:
The love the king knows I bear him answers him.

KING AHASUERUS:
Tell me all and thus prove your love.
[*Silence.*]
Your silence spawns wicked forms in me,
Shapes too hideous to utter.

ESTHER: The king does not trust his Esther…

KING AHASUERUS:
These clawing things soon will slip their leash;
Speak quickly now.

ESTHER: If the king loved me –

KING AHASUERUS: You know it!

ESTHER:
What a limp and lifeless thing is love
Unbraced by trust.

KING AHASUERUS:
You would divert me with beguiling words –
The way of specious women.
[*Pause.*]
Though your secret were enough to cave the hearts

Act Three

Of lesser men, yet, Esther, might my love for you
Wring forgiveness from wrath, and from shock milk mercy.
[*Pause.*]
Will you not speak?
[*Silence.*]
Naught hinders me from dragging forth the man
And to the rack's cruel ravage consigning him.

ESTHER: Fairest reward for fairest deed…

KING AHASUERUS:
I must know what I must know!
[*Pause.*]
But if I hurled him to the rack and said,
'Stretch this man of what the king would know,
For the king's heifer will not speak,' is this not
Ahasuerus fallen at Vashti's feet again?
Should I let myself be proverbed? Have men
Wag their heads at me and say, 'Here comes he
Who rules men and kings with power that shrinks
Before his lowing heifers'?
[*Pause.*]
Ahasuerus… Ahasuerus…
The cedar that would sweep the startled skies!
Should such loftiness to swipe of Persian wench
Now fall? Nor now, nor ever!
[*His temper flames.*]

Disgorge your secrets, wench! Tell me what I must
  know!
[*He draws his dagger, and smashing things in his way,
flies at* ESTHER.]
Speak – or perish! Speak! Speak!
[ESTHER, *stumbling, falling, flees from him and
manages to escape from the lounge. The King goes
after her.*]
[*Offstage*] Return, wench! Return!
[*Slight pause.*]
Ah, Haman, I see your gaze! Come!
[*Re-enter the King trailed by* HAMAN.]
There is a silence so very silent
'Tis the very clamour that unmans the mind.
Perish all silence therefore! – and soak me sweet
In pleasing words…

HAMAN:
I do suspect that my king today,
For reasons sealed in mystery's darkling breast,
Has barred himself from the joys of grape-rich cup.

KING AHASUERUS: To wine, then! To wine!
[*Sounds the gong for Servants. Enter Servants.*]
Unhoard the wine and swell the cups!
[*Servants hastily serve wine, refilling quickly quaffed
goblets before leaving at the King's behest.*]

HAMAN [*drinking*]: Your wine, as ever, O king,
Makes Persia's finest wine but wormwood sap;

Yet wormwood swilled in the king's beatific presence,
To Haman's tongue is fine and sweetest wine.

KING AHASUERUS:
This trilling in my ear goes well with my wine…
[*Drinks.*]
Does all, Haman, go well with the realm?

HAMAN:
The realm must go well for the king lives.
And if any in the realm presume, O king,
To go other than well, then as with the stomach
That runs sickly to retch, souring the wine
That in the goblet was sweet, a purging,
I think, O king, is surest remedy.

KING AHASUERUS:
Ah, happy man! You do not, like I, know any
Who taints and sours the goblet's sweetness…
[*He sounds summoning gong for an Attendant.*]

HAMAN:
That I do, O king! A certain people
Glut and foul the stomach to heaving.
[*Enter* HARBONA.]

KING AHASUERUS:
Harbona, fetch forth the queen!
                    [*Exit* HARBONA.

HAMAN: They scorn Persia's ways,
And by their wicked and fractious rebelliousness
Drip the realm bellyful with killing bile.
The king's dominion cries a purging of them.

KING AHASUERUS:
You are chief minister, the empire's health
To you entrusted; do what duty must do.

HAMAN: Extermination…
A decree to kill, slay, annihilate…
Only total purging will be true cure –
And I, O king, to bear the cost, will pay
Ten thousand silver talents into royal purse.
[*Pause. The King is lost in thought.*]
My king…

KING AHASUERUS: What, Haman?

HAMAN:
The purging – I will bear the cost, my king.

KING AHASUERUS:
Beggar me not with your zeal –
Keep your money and do your duty!
[*He slips off his signet ring and gives it to* HAMAN.]
Here – the king's seal for your purge…
And for mine, nothing but a sweeping word…
Go, Haman, and do what in your eyes is right.
Go!

Act Three

HAMAN:
The king's realm, like the king, will live for ever!
Live for ever, O king! Live for ever!
                              [*Exit.*
[*Enter* HARBONA.]

HARBONA: The Queen Esther!
[*Enter* ESTHER *flanked by* HATHACH *and*
MANSUR. *The King waves all out so that he is alone
with* ESTHER.]

KING AHASUERUS:
Esther, one last time I ask of you – speak.
[*Silence. The King waits, fuming.*]
Will you not speak?
[*Silence still.*]
No more, then!
[ESTHER *makes as though to speak.*]
Will you speak?
[*Silence.*]
No?
[*Silence.*]
No more, then! No more!
Nor ever before me cast yourself!
No more think to see this face! No more!
No more! Till I, in the day of new device,
Do summon you forth to lift your tongue
And rid your heart of dark and dragon deeds!
Go now! Sight be purged of you! Begone! Go! Go!

[*He kicks and hurls her out. Sounds gong. Enter Attendants.*]
[*To Attendants*] The king repairs to his lair.
You know the law and it is my command:
Who approaches the king unbidden dies!
                    [*He storms out.*]

          Curtain.

        Intermission.

Act Four

Scene 1.—HAMAN'S *house. The living room.*

The muted sound of lamentation pervades. Enter HAMAN *and* ZERESH. HAMAN *is chortling happily away.*

ZERESH:
Bilbo! Look to the doors! Seal the windows!
Seal all! Fade this draught of lamentation
Which grates even the pillars herein to gnashing!
[*To* HAMAN] What I endured without, let none, nor man,
Nor prince, nor beast, with it roil me within.
O such wailing! Has ever city,
In former times or now, in distant climes
Or regions near, seen such a plague of mourning?
How they thrashed as one in torment avowed
To batter limbs disowned, disjoined from life!
[*She goes to the door.*]
Bilbo! Lift your shanks! Still the sound! Now!
Lest I dissolve to drip of febrile madness!

HAMAN: Sweet, sweet music.

ZERESH: Bilbo!

HAMAN:
Did song ever serenade the ear's terrace
With sweeter melody or tone harmonious?

ZERESH:
Bilbo! Seal this house of dirge! Bilbo!

BILBO [*offstage*]:
The servants, at my nod, jump to it, my mistress!
[*Doors slam, and the noise abates.*]

ZERESH [*to* HAMAN]: What overthrow of reason
So makes you rattle in your seat with joy?

HAMAN: Did you not see him?

ZERESH: Who?

HAMAN: Mordecai.

ZERESH: Mordecai?

HAMAN: Porter at the king's gate.

ZERESH: I know him not.

HAMAN:
'Tis as well, for you might have pitied him,
Or pitied him not, not discerning him:
A mask of blood wore he on his face

From violence of his own hands, and on his form
A fog of dust and ashes, scarlet striped
From much self-gashing. [*He laughs.*]

ZERESH:
I could not, a hundred times surveying,
Discern any in that sea of dust and bruise –
What a flood of them swept the square!
None ever did tell me the Jews of Susa
Were of number to stretch the eye to bleeding.
Yet it was the tremor of their wailing
That most assaulted my calm, and oft I feared
The air would crack from it and rain us dead
With hailstone tears.
[*Pause.*]
But what moved the king to such damning decree?

HAMAN: I.
[*Pause.* ZERESH *in questioning shock.*]
Not the king, but I,
Moved myself to motion long intended
And long restrained.
[*He roars with laughter.*]
Now, Zeresh, have I let fall my dark designs.
My dream is done, my life appeased, my yearning fed!

ZERESH: You... Haman?

HAMAN: Ay.
[*Pause.*]

I and the lot I cast for a destruction
In time's broad scroll unequalled.

ZERESH: Haman…

HAMAN: No. Mordecai. Mordecai offended me.

ZERESH: Mordecai…

HAMAN:
He would not bow; now he eats dust, snorts dirt,
And snaffles sandy ground. He grovels and gnashes,
Befogged by ashes, who once was bright with pride:
Too proud to bow to Haman.

ZERESH: For one man…

HAMAN:
I sought to trap a nation, but trapped a man,
One man only, but he caught me my nation:
Put Jew squashed in my palm.

ZERESH: This hatred you bear the Jew…

HAMAN:
Fear it! And fear, too, Haman's patience!
Let all men fear my patience! In humiliation
I was patient and raged not to the king
To have my transgressor hanged, but in venom
Multiplied the wrong till at my feet
It gave me a nation abased, and in my palm

Act Four

A yearning appeased. Zeresh, behold me well!
Behold me! See! I stand at history's door,
Poised to incurse burnished remembrance
As he who from the list of living nations
Peeled off the name of Jew, so that men
Should scour the earth for Jew and find him not.

ZERESH: Hatred so brimming
Is the acid that eats its own cup.

HAMAN [*heedless*]:
A bowl heavy with device I nursed
Till chance lent me ladle to stir my smouldering brew.
[*He goes to the door.*]
Bilbo! Send quickly for my friends!
Let all this day come early to Haman's court;
There is much roistering to pursue,
Much merriment to toil and labour at,
And we must early start or else disrobe the night.

ZERESH:
One question, my lord; one question answer me
Before you swing to the hoist of night's plans.

HAMAN: Yes?

ZERESH:
Why mark you so this tribe with rabid hate?

HAMAN: Because they are Jew.

ZERESH: Yes, but why hate you the Jew so?
[*Long pause.*]

HAMAN: Because they are Jew.
[*His great laughter rents the air. Lights fade.*]

Scene 2.—*The Queen's chamber.*

ESTHER *paces the room anxiously. Present are* HALALISA *and* LEILA.

ESTHER: Mansur!

MANSUR [*offstage*]: My queen!
[*Enter* MANSUR.]

ESTHER: What keeps Hathach so long?

MANSUR:
But my lady does not understand – the throng,
Packed locust-thick, annuls all path and hope of air.

ESTHER:
I must have news that unveils this madness!

MANSUR:
A madness to which nothing before compares, my queen.
Their gale of frenzy mocks a storm's upheaval
And twits it idling breeze, a feeble breath.
And though Hathach's passage were unhindered,
The eagle must lend him eyes to spy

Act Four

The man Mordecai in the sea of dust
That floods the trembling square.

ESTHER:
Mordecai, 'tis said, outmourns them all,
But woe that this and not some trill of joy
Should pluck him to the eye! But go, Mansur!
Go to them and hasten news to me.
I must know the rib and soul of this lament.

MANSUR: As my lady commands.
                              [*Exit.*

ESTHER [*seeing* HALALISA'S *face*]:
Why, Halalisa! The look you wear…
Leila, and you too?
[*Pause.*]
Here, Halalisa…
[*Holds a hairbrush to her.*]
[ESTHER *sits by a mirror.* HALALISA *begins to brush her hair but soon starts to cry.*]
Halalisa… What troubles you?

HALALISA: Your hair…

ESTHER: My hair?

HALALISA:
Your hair has lost its sheen, my queen.

ESTHER [*examining her hair*]:
I see but nothing amiss…

HALALISA: All is amiss! Amiss and very wrong!
[*Her weeping intensifies.*]

ESTHER: Halalisa… Halalisa…
Soft now, Lisa, soft!
[LEILA *joins her to console* HALALISA.]
Leila, do you know what ails her so?

LEILA:
For days you have thrown meat to scorn…

ESTHER: Will she not eat?

LEILA: Not her, my lady. You.

ESTHER: Me?

LEILA:
And have little known the touch of sleep…

HALALISA: In the dark we hear you cry!

LEILA:
But you have sealed your lips from us
And left us spent in speechless sorrow;
Our eyes are haunted yellow with strange grief:
We mourn and mourn and know not why we mourn.

HALALISA: You tell us nothing – nothing…

Act Four

LEILA: Melancholy has stolen in here…

HALALISA:
We languish with you, my lady,
We faint, we die; yet you shut us off,
Nor will break this dreadful hush.

LEILA:
Laughter has died; Joy has left her corner…
[*Pause.*]

HALALISA: My lady?
[ESTHER *does not answer but looks at her questioningly.*]
[*Persisting*] My lady?

ESTHER: Halalisa, speak.

HALALISA:
Will my lady shun her silence this once
And with answer calm my throbbing heart,
Telling me what I fain would know?
[*Slight pause.*]

ESTHER: Ask.

HALALISA:
The news of Jewish grief, of no concern to us,
No concern at all, caught the queen fast
In so fitful a tremor for cure;
Why has my lady not with matching care

Sought to stem her own malaise which in deepest
  gloom
Sinks the queen and all her swans with her?
[*Enter* HATHACH *and* MANSUR.]

ESTHER: Hathach!

HATHACH: My queen!

ESTHER: What, Hathach?

HATHACH: My queen!

ESTHER: What?

HATHACH: 'Tis for my lady's ears alone.

ESTHER: Speak!

HATHACH:
Dare I assault this place, wound this gentle air?

ESTHER [*sighting a scroll in his hand*]:
What thing is that you bear?

HATHACH: A royal edict – he bade me show you.
[*He gives her the annihilation edict and she reads it.*]

ESTHER:
To kill, slay, annihilate all Jews…
To kill, slay, annihilate all Jews?
This – the king…?

HATHACH: Not the king. Haman.

ESTHER: Haman?

HATHACH:
In darkened corners, with shrouded figures,
Haman cast the lot for Jewish death.

ESTHER: Haman…

HATHACH:
Author of destruction, doom's architect;
By guile winning the king's unprobing assent.

ESTHER:
To kill, slay, annihilate… Can this be?

HATHACH: My lady…

ESTHER: To annihilate… Annihilate…

HATHACH: My lady…

ESTHER: All Jews…

HATHACH: My lady, Mordecai –

ESTHER: Mordecai! What says Mordecai?

HATHACH:
Mordecai requests the queen to go –
Before the day decreed for slaughter –

To go to the king, and for Jewish life
To intercede, pleading, if need be,
Her very blood for mercy.

ESTHER:
To go before the king – for mercy?

HATHACH:
He bade me say these words: 'Think not, Esther,
By strength of royal seat alone of all the Jews
To find escape. Hold your peace and perish –
Perish, Esther, with all your father's line –
But though many be slain, not all Jews shall fall,
For deliverance surely shall rise from other sphere –
Surely shall rise! – and then shall shame attend your name,
For who knows but you've come to royal seat
For such a time as this.'

ESTHER: To go before the king…
[*Pause.*]
No… No… I cannot… The king sits in sanctum…
I cannot… No! From the king's presence I was cast
In pain of my life, nor have seen his face
Thirty days! The world – the world and all men know
Any who goes to him unbidden dies!
[*Pause.*]
No… No… I cannot do it… No!
[*Pause.*]

Act Four

Hathach, return to Mordecai. Tell him no,
I cannot do what he asks of me; I cannot!

HATHACH: As my lady commands.
                              [*Exit.*
[*Long pause.*]

ESTHER: Mansur! Fetch Hathach back! Fly!
                              [*Exit* MANSUR.
[*Silence.* ESTHER *looks at her maids intently, in turns. They cannot return her gaze and fall away. She stares afar; here, there; her anguish pulsating through her very flesh.* HATHACH *and* MANSUR *re-enter.*]
[*To* HATHACH]
What were his words? Give me his words!

HATHACH: 'Think not, Esther –'

ESTHER:
No! No! His plea's end – 'Who knows…'

HATHACH:
'For who knows but you've come to royal seat
For such a time as this.'

ESTHER: Yes…
[*Pause.*]
Again, Hathach!

HATHACH: 'For who knows –'

ESTHER [*stopping him*]: Yes! Yes! Yes!
[*Pause.*]
'For such a time as this…' Were those his words?
'For such a time as this…' His words, Hathach?
His very words? 'For such a time as this…'
'For such a time as this…'
[*She covers her face a while then looks up, glassy-eyed.*]
My maids and I, three days long, will fast,
Nor eating, nor drinking, night or day.
Then will I before the king throw myself
Though it defies the law and damns his very word.
And if I perish, I perish.
[*Pause. Lights begin to fade.*]
If I perish, I perish.
[*Lights fade.*]

Scene 3.—*The palace. Antechamber to the Queen's room.*

MANSUR *alone, but* HATHACH *presently stumbles in.*

MANSUR: Hathach!
Did he with mercy greet the impetuous entry?
Did he raise the royal sceptre? Hathach!
[HATHACH, *abstracted, slowly shakes his head.*]
Alas! We are undone!

HATHACH: Lies! All lies! Rootless rumours!

Act Four

MANSUR: Hathach?

HATHACH:
With these eyes did I see General Tabriz,
His neck upon his shoulders, at court, dusky,
Seated, waiting, his fine and noble head
Upon his stout and worthy neck.

MANSUR: He is alive, then?

HATHACH: Alive and well.

MANSUR:
Then there is hope yet for the queen!

HATHACH: What hope? The good general,
Unhurt by scourge of royal wrath lives
Because, and only because, his master
Now is restraint, his good counsel caution,
Fencing him strong from the sanctum walls.
If he errs and ventures in unbidden
He good as snuffs his own life, for royal temper
Now truly skirts the edge of mad unreason.

MANSUR: Is the king still no better?

HATHACH:
This day of days is his rage a killing beast.
No life by him is safe; death stalks the sanctum.
They die who move false, nor matters he is Tabriz

By growing reports of Greek incursion
Wearied to rash and fatal impatience.

MANSUR: Or the queen?

HATHACH:
Or the queen. Mansur, will you stand – will I –
And watch the queen pop headlong into death's jaws?

MANSUR: Is there aught we can do?

HATHACH: We can act!

MANSUR: Ay, but how?

HATHACH:
Are we not the queen's guards, her chief guards?
Is her very life not to us entrusted?
We must do what falls on us to do.

MANSUR: Listen! I think they come.

HATHACH: I hear nothing.

MANSUR: But if they come?

HATHACH: We must stop her!

MANSUR:
Will you lay your hands on the queen?

HATHACH:
Not I. Her maids – Halalisa, Leila, Lolithe.
They can do what we cannot do.

MANSUR:
Have you not seen them? Three days of fasting
And all their fight is gone. They are like sheep
Who dare bleat their shepherd no cry.

HATHACH:
Then it falls on us alone to do all.
Perhaps – perhaps we may reason with her;
Where force dare not walk, reason oft may venture.
We must reason with her, raise winning pleas.

MANSUR: She has laid a banquet for the king.

HATHACH: A banquet?

MANSUR:
Madness... Royal madness...
No less a thing askew by frame of royalty.
[*Listening closely*] I think they come.

HATHACH:
They may come, but here they stop and return.
They will not pass on. I am hard resolved.

MANSUR: And I with you.
[*They wait.*]

HATHACH: Do they not come?

MANSUR: Hush!
[*Pause.*]

HATHACH: They do not come.

MANSUR: They will.
[*Pause.*]

HATHACH: What think you of Hegai?

MANSUR: Hegai?

HATHACH: Yes, Hegai.

MANSUR: Why? What must I think of him?

HATHACH:
Do you not see? In all the serving household
Who, in our noble queen's sight, stands highest?
Whose merest presence to hearing rouses
Unheeding ears, popping off their stoppers?
Whose tongue, schooled deep in reason's byways,
Is such a ramp of persuasion that by his
Mine is but a peasant's rustic trowel?

MANSUR:
The queen and her stricken maids come now;
We have not time for Hegai.

Act Four

HATHACH:
We must chance it – fetch him! Go with wings!

MANSUR: No! I go nowhere. You go!
Would you deny me my last look queenward?

HATHACH: But go and it will be looks aplenty.

MANSUR: I go nowhere.
Do you boast a love greater than mine
That you should stay to see her one last time
And I lope off and never see her more?

HATHACH:
I plead no love greater than yours, Mansur,
Nor do I plead a love greater than lives
In the heart of every man and maid
Who within these walls earns a keep,
And who, for the queen, would lay down life.
But I make this plea: the queen shall not –
And I thunder it forth – the queen shall not,
While Hathach remains her chief of guard,
Cross yonder threshold to dally or date
This day with death. I, Hathach, say it!
[*Pause.*]
Mansur, as my resolve roots me here,
Should not your love oil you quick to Hegai?

MANSUR: You will restrain her?

HATHACH: I have said it.

MANSUR: I go, then.

HATHACH:
Go quick! And return with Hegai to find me here,
Barring the queen, and rock-ridge immovable.

MANSUR: I set my trust upon your word.

HATHACH: Quick!
[*Exit* MANSUR.
[HATHACH *listens, tense. Moves stealthily towards the queen's chamber door. Stops. Listens. Suddenly* MANSUR *returns.*]
Mansur!

MANSUR: It cannot be done.

HATHACH: What!

MANSUR: The vow!

HATHACH: Her life depends on us! Go!

MANSUR: Do you forget?
We swore silence to all our ears had heard!

HATHACH:
Fetch Hegai! Only he can dissuade her. Go!

Act Four

MANSUR:
When Hegai asks why, what will Mansur say?

HATHACH:
The queen goes to her death – tell him!
Tell him what you will, but bring him here!

MANSUR:
I swore to the queen and thus sealed my lips.
Though your vow, Hathach, be but a belch to you,
Mine binds and keeps me fast in honour's chains.

HATHACH:
O what a fool! What a simp and senseless fool!

MANSUR: Do my ears hear right?

HATHACH: Fool! Fool!

MANSUR:
Words that spell your death – brace your lance!

HATHACH:
No! I will not fight – nor cackle even!
Keep your ire till the queen from death is swayed;
That done, then I'm yours.
[*Brooding silence.*]
I can close her path, but only for a time.
If her swaying must exceed piddling time
She must have words more than I know to give.
Mansur, I will go myself to Hegai.

MANSUR: You go a shade late. See –
[*Enter* ESTHER *accompanied by* HALALISA *and* LEILA.]

HATHACH: My lady!

MANSUR: My queen!

ESTHER:
Hathach and Mansur – guards and faithful friends
Who by my sides have served with loyal hearts,
I note you well and know you know it;
I am thus becalmed though squall clips my speech.
If I return, 'tis well; if no, no worse.
Farewell then, my friends; my good thanks to you.

HATHACH [*throwing himself at her feet*]:
Never, my lady!

ESTHER: What means this?

HATHACH:
'Tis not for me, my queen, to judge your cause
Or seek to arbitrate it right or wrong,
But will my queen not lift her gaze and see
That her timing joins calamity's scheme
To unleash and torrent death her way?
Will the queen not delay her cause awhile
To see what lease new days perchance might bring?
Surely any day but this – any day! –

Will yield fairer fruit than this reek of death
That so despoils this day!

MANSUR:
We fear, my lady; where you seek to tread
Today houses death's severing blade.
[ESTHER *sidesteps* HATHACH.]

ESTHER:
The blade you speak of did form my jail bars
These three and thirty days: I know its fear.
Now, this day, for good or ill, life or death,
I break its bars, defy to death its hold.
[HATHACH *throws himself again before her.*]

HATHACH: We beseech you, O queen!
Delay your cause; hold it a day or two…

ESTHER [*sidestepping*]: No more of this, Hathach.

MANSUR:
We fear what toll three days' fasting, O queen,
Has drawn from you.

HATHACH [*rising*]:
Will the queen not first be nourished?

MANSUR:
And then tomorrow or any day hereafter…

HATHACH:
I warrant the queen today is too weak.

ESTHER:
Too weak, yes; too weak to fling words abroad,
But strong enough to do what I must do.
[*To Maids*] Halalisa, Leila, hold yourselves firm.
Leila, do you weep? Oh Leila… Come now…
Wipe your tears… Leila, come, come…
Wipe your tears…
[HATHACH *hulks in front of her.*]

HATHACH: O queen, we cannot let you go.

ESTHER:
Out of my way, Hathach. Leave. Leave now.
[HATHACH *does not move.*]
Out, I say!
[HATHACH *still does not move. Long, menacing silence. Then* HATHACH, *as though having succumbed, turns and walks towards exit.* ESTHER *turns to her Maids.*]
Come now… Leila… No more tears now… Leila…
Halalisa, rise; rise, my swan… Come, come…
Be strong for me. Come…
[*Turning round,* ESTHER *is shocked to find that* HATHACH *is now blocking the doorway. But she walks towards him, though cautiously. When she is near,* HATHACH *suddenly raises his lance. It is a*

Act Four

barring gesture, not meant to be menacing, but menacing still.]
You dare…?

HATHACH:
I dare do all that my duty commands.
[Long, tense silence.]

ESTHER [*of a sudden*]:
Mansur! Come! I command you – clear my path!
[MANSUR *slowly approaches* HATHACH. HATHACH *is unsure of him. But* MANSUR, *standing by* HATHACH, *suddenly adopts* HATHACH'S *stance and forms a complete lance-guard with him to bar* ESTHER.]

MANSUR: I must do my duty, too.
[Silence. MANSUR *is so tense he is trembling.]*

ESTHER: Mansur, you defy me?
[Silence. Then MANSUR *crumbles and falls away.]*

MANSUR: Oh, Hathach, I cannot do this.
[It is only a few moments before HATHACH, *undermined by* MANSUR'S *defeat, himself succumbs.]*

HATHACH [*yielding way*]: It is finished, then!
[He hurls his lance to the floor. ESTHER *and her Maids leave. Silence. Enter* LOLITHE.]

LOLITHE: Is my queen gone? Ah, woe is me!

MANSUR: You trudge not alone, Lolithe, in woe.

LOLITHE: Woe! Woe is me!

MANSUR:
Henceforth call this house sepulchre, the lodge of dirge,
And us the living dead.

LOLITHE [*grasping miserably at* HATHACH]:
Hathach…

HATHACH: What have I to do with you?

LOLITHE [*weeping*]:
Call me wretched! Call me worse than wretched!

HATHACH:
How did wretchedness leave us to find only you?

LOLITHE:
'Twas only me did this wicked thing –
Who did betray the queen.

MANSUR: What is this you say, Lolithe?

LOLITHE:
I betrayed the queen; I supped and broke the fast.

HATHACH: You broke the fast?

LOLITHE:
On the second day of our closeting,
Hunger's pangs on me laid such conquering siege
That when none watched I did slip away to sup.

HATHACH:
If there was hope, that hope is lost and gone.
Away from me, Lolithe! Away! Begone!
Mansur, this new thing, though an ill-tiding,
Duty bids me hasten off to the queen.
                                      [*Exit.*

MANSUR:
Why, what good? And he goes too late I fear;
Naught is his but to stand in dumb dismay
If he meets the three in sanctum sphere –
In court or lounge, or place surrounding,
Where silence, by law, must reign unquelled.

LOLITHE:
Why could not I tarry a little day –
One more day for my queen? Why? Why?

MANSUR:
Private sorrow to universal grief
Now must yield, Lolithe.

LOLITHE: I am undone.

MANSUR: We all are, this way or that.

LOLITHE:
Wretched me! Wretched, wretched me!
Who could not tarry a little day!

MANSUR:
Had you tarried to your heart's content,
Not your belly's, all your tarrying still
Would have been in vain. When death calls royalty,
They sweep to it with mad and royal rush,
And not all the clamour of eunuch slaves,
Or all a gibbering maid's wailing,
Will deny the flood its torrenting.
[*A scream, muffled by walls and distance, but potently audible, carries to them.*]
What now is that?

LOLITHE: Ah! My mistress! Alas! Alas! Alas!
[*She thrashes around hysterically.*]

MANSUR: What, Lolithe! Hold!

LOLITHE:
My mistress! And none but I did this deed!

MANSUR: Hold!

LOLITHE [*tearing at her throat and pummelling her stomach*]:
I'll gouge this gorging thing yet! You! – and you!

MANSUR: Lolithe!

Act Four

LOLITHE:
Ah! Tongue that did sneak to eat – I pluck you!

MANSUR: Madness!

LOLITHE [*dashing herself to the ground*]:
Bereave the hour that bore me, rag maid of unrestraint!

MANSUR: Forbear! Would you destroy yourself?

LOLITHE [*flinging herself down again*]:
Bereave the hour and let me die!

MANSUR: Mindless remorse! Hold!

LOLITHE: Woe! Woe!

MANSUR [*grabbing hold of her*]: Soft now – Soft!
Would you wound, destroy yourself? What vantage
 gain,
But for a brief moment cast grief's eye on dross,
Feeding it there with zeal and angry flip
To send it blazing to gaze again on gold?
[*Re-enter* HATHACH *bearing a woman in his arms.*]

LOLITHE [*leaping to* HATHACH]: My lady!

HATHACH: 'Tis Halalisa.
[*He places her on a couch.*]

LOLITHE: Halalisa?

MANSUR:
What bestirs this pool to endless ripple?

HATHACH:
Who can say what vision she saw and screamed,
And I but caught her as she fell in faint.
[*Halalisa wakens.*]

MANSUR: She stirs…

HALALISA: My lady… Where is my lady?

HATHACH: Gone.

HALALISA: Gone? Where?

HATHACH: Into the midst and mist of death.

HALALISA: My lady!
[*She leaps up and runs off.*]

LOLITHE: Halalisa, wait!
[*She goes after her.*]

HATHACH:
I have done all. Who is he can do more?

MANSUR:
The day bays for blood and will not rest.
O noblest of ladies! Would now that beauty,
In you so pure and true, could be your help!
Or deliverance come from that fragrant goodness

That so freely from you gave sweetened breath
To even these dumb walls!
[*Lights fade.*]

Scene 4.—*The palace. The King's sanctum.*

The King is fretfully pacing the stairs of the raised dais on which his throne sits. Except for two Servants who stand by his throne to fan him, all others present – Attendants, Musicians, Scribes, the Physician – are below. The Musicians fill the chamber with soft melodious music.

KING AHASUERUS:
Peace! Peace! I will have more than this strumming
You say ever has been the cure of kings!
[*Music ceases. Pause.*]

PHYSICIAN: Great king –

KING AHASUERUS:
Tongues are for speaking. Speak!

PHYSICIAN:
Great king, as balm for kingly afflictions,
The fruit of minstrelsy surpasses all potions –
And I say this though none commingles a potion
Better than I. If the king would but abide
Its softening virtues a little longer…

KING AHASUERUS:
No! I will have a true remedy!
Your potions and herbs are but belly bloating,
Your music a jarring jag jar!
Now strum no more! Nor commingle aught
Save to commingle your brain to addle me peace
To quench this raging in my temple,
This boiling in my eyes! See this heart?
No, it is here – No, here! – It is here!
It mocks me! It beats from left to right,
From right to left – wheresoever it pleases!
Wings of fury, cease! Cease!
[*A gong sounds at the double-doors joining inner court to sanctum. They open.*]
Does any dare…?
[*At first no one, then a figure rushes in, immediately falling prostrate in homage.*]
Stand! Show your face and die!
[*The figure rises.*]
Tabriz! You?

TABRIZ: My king…

KING AHASUERUS:
You dare defy me? The law? Tabriz?

TABRIZ:
I waited, O king, till duty bade me rise
And cast down fear to love's treading feet.

Act Four

KING AHASUERUS: You die!

TABRIZ:
My king, the Greeks invade!
Hellene's sons swarm the western posts!
Cilicia buckles. The realm is threatened, my lord!

KING AHASUERUS:
When the mighty Tabriz babbles, when the pride
Of Persia's army becomes a yodelling infant,
When men elect to scorn the king's command,
The realm, alas, knows the snarl of threat.
[*Pause.*]
Tabriz, your lieutenant Akabah,
I do not recall is wed to puerile splutter.
Even now as I speak, my words transfer your sword
To his hand to sweep, without first babbling the king,
Hellene's sons back to festering Aegean's isles.
He will do what you would not, and live;
And you, die…

TABRIZ:
Any man worth his rank and honour, O king,
Would have done as I, had he, running with love
And courage, these reasons which to the king
I fain would explain…

KING AHASUERUS:
No more! I have spoken! You die!

TABRIZ: Great king,
At Hellespont, in youth's fair dawning,
Back to back in bloody fray, who, O king,
Stood with you when no brother would, and with battle-axe
And bleeding sword, did heave when you did heave,
Did strike when you did strike, smote when you smote,
Brandishing when you brandished, nor tiring once,
Nor flinching ever, till clashing steel made ringing song
Of battle's bloody air, and Persia's fainting men,
Happy always for song, fainted no more,
But resurged in thunder strokes that soon made
Hellene's routers Hellene's routed,
And set Persia's name striding gory proud
Into gallant history's timeless fields?
Who was it stood with you and did this thing?
Who, O king?

KING AHASUERUS:
You it was – who yourself threw yourself
This day into death's unhappy court.
Choose therefore your manner of dying
And shuffle verbiage no more! Choose!

TABRIZ: My king,
I fear not death nor flinch from night's grave call,
Yet duty so deep is in me ingrained
It has eyes to see that the king tomorrow,

When this passing malady has fled his sight,
Will say 'Would Tabriz had lived to serve me
As ever he did; to honour me
As was his happy wont. Would someone that day
Had stayed my hand!' Therefore does my duty say:
Stay your hand, O king, and render mercy;
Render mercy, O great king!

KING AHASUERUS: Mercy! Had I mercy to bestow,
Think I first would not bestow it on myself?
And on my brow raise yon sceptre and say,
'Quench! You burning thing! Quench! Burn not! Burn no more!'?
But no more! No more be said than this:
Who ventures here, who comes unbidden dies!
Nor will I ever from this word swerve,
Though himself who accosts these portals
Were mightiest Darius, that greatly revered king,
Beloved sire of mine, whose memory...
Whose memory... Oh, I care not! Nothing now is true!
Nothing beloved or dear! All is dry dust, dead grit!
No, not anything, nor anyone,
Will from this word sway me: Who defies me dies!
Who enters is undone!
[*Gong sounds, and the sanctum doors open.*]
What! Who?
[*All eyes rivet to the doors in shock, but no one enters. Utter silence. Then a light from without trails in, but*

still no one. Suddenly ESTHER *appears, standing barely inside the chamber.*]
Esther!
[*The doors shut behind her. She does not speak. Silence. King and queen cast burning looks at each other.* ESTHER *makes no gesture of homage. A long moment, then the King half turns his back to her.*]
You die!
[ESTHER *sways and begins to fall, uttering a swooning sound which causes the King to turn.*]

TABRIZ: Hold her there! She falls!

KING AHASUERUS: Let none touch her!
[ESTHER *falls. Unhurriedly the King descends the dais and goes to the fallen figure.*]
Would any presume to touch the queen –
Profane the person of my anointed one?
[*He gathers her up in his arms and walks back towards the dais.*]
Though I have given her over to death,
Yet she is queen.

PHYSICIAN [*approaching*]:
My lord the king, if I may…

KING AHASUERUS: Physician, away!
To what end will you look to her,
Seeing death is her portion?
[*Climbing with slow and ponderous steps, he stops halfway and bends to the inert form.*]

Act Four

Oh Esther... Esther... Esther...
[*He continues up the dais.*]
[*At the top*]
Bring the queen a couch! Physician, attend the queen!
Minstrels, burst forth minstrelsy! Strike sweet,
   pleasing tones!
Weave my queen a couch of melody!
[*A couch is brought and music fills the chamber as the queen is attended to. Presently she stirs.*]
[*Clearing the dais*] Away now! Away!

ESTHER [*still befuddled*]:
What? My lord? My king...

KING AHASUERUS:
Esther, my precious! Esther...
[*He reaches for his sceptre and touches her with the tip*]
Live, my queen; live!

ESTHER [*flinging her arms round his neck*]:
Oh, my lord and king... My lord and king...

KING AHASUERUS: My precious... My Esther...
[*After a while he disengages himself and steps back away from her.*]
That I may behold my queen...
These eyes – was it not for this they hurt,
Aching to behold fair beauty's own eyes?
[*Pause.*]

Wondrously arrayed with gifts of healing
Have you come, my beloved, my precious, my queen...
My heart beats soft now, 'tis whole and content;
Gentle peace lays cooling hands on my brow,
And in my eyes dew freshness sprinkles sweet surcease;
That the spark and charge of my distemper
Should be the channel now of my healing...
[*Seeing she has begun to weep*]
Ah, my heart, do you weep?
Wherefore do you weep? Why, Esther? Why, my queen?

ESTHER: Relief delights
To make a silly weeping thing of me.
[*Pause.*]
And yet, my lord, that certain matter
The king desired to know of me...

KING AHASUERUS:
No, speak not of that matter.
This day I rejoice only that my heart
Has come back to me: wholeness again is mine.

ESTHER:
Yet if I may ask the king a request
And lay a petition before my gentle lord...

Act Four

KING AHASUERUS:
Ask and it is yours, my Esther.
No good thing will I withhold from you.
To the very half of my kingdom –
It is yours if you but ask.

ESTHER: If my good lord
Will come to a banquet I have prepared…

KING AHASUERUS: A banquet?

ESTHER:
I request, too, the company of Lord Haman.

KING AHASUERUS: A banquet?

ESTHER:
I shall make my request there, my king;
Haman sitting with the king in feast
At my petition's table.

KING AHASUERUS:
Esther, like Esther, ever grace will mirror –
And style and poise and sweet enigma's charm!
So be it: to wine, then! To venison!
To sweet meats! To merriment and good cheer!
My beloved, my fair and precious jewel,
How my soul has longed to laugh and dine with you!
Ho there! Send speedy summons to Haman!
An urgent chariot! An escort of haste!
True! Nothing glads the heart like sweet surprise,

Or so piques the palate as a riddling feast.
Tabriz, say, what keeps you here? See my sceptre's
　　tip –
Begone to duty's post and live a hundred years!

TABRIZ [*prostrating*]: My most gracious lord!

ATTENDANTS: Greatest of kings! Live for ever!

KING AHASUERUS:
And let the good earth live! My Esther, come.
See, your fragrance cures the world of tight faces;
How they smile now with wide and bursting hearts!
Lead me, my queen, I'm yours.
　　　　　　　　[*Exeunt King and* ESTHER. *Curtain.*

Act Five

Scene 1.—HAMAN'S *house. The living room.*

BILBO, *intoxicated, pours himself more of his master's wine. At the sound of approach he makes a fumbling attempt to conceal his mischief.*

MIHESO [*offstage*]: Bilbo!

BILBO: Miheso…

MIHESO [*still offstage*]: Bilbo! Bilbo!

BILBO [*rattling*]:
Miheso, Miheso, Miheso… Miheso…
'Tis tears from the weeping vine that weeps no more.
[*Enter* MIHESO.]

MIHESO: Bilbo! I who have forsworn the vine
Will in Queen Esther's tribute break my vow.

BILBO:
To Esther! To Esther! To great Queen Esther!
[*He passes* MIHESO *some wine.*]
Drink slowly, Miheso…

Let the tongue in leisured swirls swim its length.
Haman swills to the king's wine and we to Haman's.
[*Laughs.*]

MIHESO:
'Tis to the queen's wine the master swills:
'Tis Esther's banquet; the king, no less than Haman,
Attending as summoned guest.

BILBO:
'Tis a raising! 'Tis a raising for Haman!
Of nobles, he alone called to Esther's feast –
'Tis a joyous raising! And we with him are raised
In lifting wine! To Haman! To Esther!
Ay to Esther! To Esther! To great Queen Esther!
From whose hand the great eat, and we drink!

MIHESO:
But by what charm has she done this thing?
Vashti, striking in time of cheer, was unspared;
Esther strikes in fevered time and walks off thick
With sheaves of mercy.

BILBO:
Beauty bears with it the spark of power,
And great beauty flames with blinding blaze.

MIHESO: Vashti, too, was great of beauty.

BILBO: Ah, but she never did learn to fly!

Act Five

MIHESO: Fly?

BILBO:
In puff of smoke. Did you not hear? 'Tis said
The doors were shut, the sanctum sealed in gall,
And then before the raging king appeared a puff –
A sudden puff of smoke – and out of it –
Flew Esther!

MIHESO [*laughing*]: Before the week is old
Persia's minstrels will wrap her fond in song.

BILBO:
And did you not hear? As she fronted the king
Her robes split in lips to uncover melody.
[*They laugh.*]
And they said…
[*Enter* SIKURU.]

SIKURU [*laughing*]: They said, they said…

BILBO: Sikuru! Sikuru!

SIKURU:
They said she stormed the doors grown to giant girth –
As tall as tallest royal palm!

BILBO: 'Tis no wonder then the king did faint!

MIHESO: Did the king faint?

BILBO: Did you not hear?
And she swept him up in cradling arm,
A cradle soft and strong and cavern deep,
And with breeze of palmy other arm
Did fan him weeping stunned to baby sleep.

SIKURU: Weeping stunned in faint?
[*They laugh. A door is heard slamming.*]

MIHESO: The master?

BILBO: No! 'Tis the wind!
The master feasts, the lady sleeps,
The servants play in merry ease…

MIHESO:
All feasts of life and love, or wine, must end.

BILBO: 'Tis the wind!
Merrily, merrily, merrily blows the merry wind…

HAMAN [*offstage*]: Zeresh! Zeresh!

SIKURU [*scampering off*]: Quick!
[*He and* MIHESO *run off.*]

BILBO [*unperturbed*]:
'Tis the master… The master…

HAMAN [*still offstage*]: Zeresh! Zeresh! Zeresh!

Act Five

BILBO: Why flee?
From good cheer perchance may come sweet uses:
Some gift in remembrance of services past,
Of loyalty firm and true… Why flee?
[*Enter* HAMAN. *His scowl swivels between* BILBO *and the pell-mell evidence of reckless carousing.* BILBO *prostrates.*]
My master, may the rush and overflow
Of your evening's sup fall full on me.

HAMAN [*grabbing an ornamental chain belt*]:
It is yours.
[*He belabours* BILBO *till the howling Servant manages to escape. Enter* ZERESH.]

ZERESH: Haman! What fury so possesses you?

HAMAN: He was there –
Sitting as though no night had slain his day!
Oh, Zeresh! Zeresh!

ZERESH: But who?

HAMAN:
With springy steps did I leave the queen's banquet,
My heart light and flighty as the evening air,
My thoughts soft as sweetest song –
And there he was! –
Sitting at the gate, calm as a cave,

Sure as the hills, unmoved, unmarred, unmastered!
Sight never so slew me, nor gaze galled me dead!

ZERESH: Mordecai?

HAMAN:
His sackcloth and ashes gone, his wailing ceased,
His silence damning, his face hard, flint-stone hard,
Stiff-wrapped and steep, defiant and damning!
Careless that all the world to me did fall
On cowed and bended knees! Oh! Zeresh!
Royal fête fled my breast, all joys and pleasures
    skipped!

ZERESH:
'Tis a peculiar man that makes my Haman cry.

HAMAN:
I'm disembowelled, ruptured! Nor have any stomach
For Queen Esther's feast again tomorrow!

ZERESH: Does the queen feast again tomorrow?

HAMAN:
She pledged the king she would tomorrow divulge
What feebleness did today abort,
And begged with deepest sighs my fellowship again.
Zeresh, though I gave her my word to go,
How can I go a-roving when a sight remains
That sickens me lame, wounds me desolate?

Act Five

What manner of man would scorn the breath of death?
What strong steel holds that man? On what rock
Stands he bold? What hand keeps his mountain firm?
I could have ripped his frame asunder!
I could have had him flayed! Quartered him! Skinned him!
Struck him down! Shredded him to tiny little strips!
I could have strung him up! Strung him up high!
So high the very stars to behold him
Fain would strain their eyes upwards and upwards
To the uttermost peaks of sightless space!

ZERESH: Then why cry to me? String him up high!

HAMAN:
And have him escape my day of slaughter?
The day I have allotted his eyes to behold
A festival of dying, a banquet of blood
And bleeding? Have him escape my destruction
Of babes and maids and the aged and juvenile Jew?
No, Zeresh! No!

ZERESH: Then sit and pine and cry,
And pine and cry and die.
[*Long pause.*]

HAMAN: I could have him strung up...

ZERESH: In the morning... and then at eventide
Visit your queen with light and merry heart.

HAMAN: On gallows high, so high…

ZERESH:
The highest a hanging ever will see –
Five and twenty feet aloft, or thirty-five,
Or forty-five, or five and fifty feet high –
Or seventy-five… Any five but fit and high!

HAMAN: And enjoy my wine at eventide
In royal ease. [*Chortling*] Yes… Yes… Zeresh…
   Zeresh…
This counsel my brain carves me lifts my head high
And stretches me full with breathless relief.
I shall hack the night into a hanging beast!
This very night, this night, I shall frame my gallows
Tall and brave and hanging hideous!
And at dawn, none other outpacing me,
Be at court for royal leave to feed my beast!
Ah, yes! Bilbo! Fetch me men stalwart and strong!
[*Begins to go.*]
Up Bilbo to town! Up and away!
Tonight – tonight we raise the beast!
                          [*Exit.*

ZERESH:
Now can a woman have some peace… Ah!
[*Lights fade.*]

Act Five

Scene 2.—*The palace. Antechamber to the King's room.*

Just after dawn. King's guard ASHANTI *hears footfalls.*

ASHANTI: Who comes? Stand! Speak!

JABUL [*offstage*]:
Jabul – inspecting the king's guard.

ASHANTI: Approach.
[*Enter* JABUL.]

JABUL: Alert as ever, Ashanti;
'Tis much to your credit. How fares the watch?

ASHANTI:
Dawn signals me to relief and to my bed;
I'm glad for such relieving mercies.

JABUL:
Tal and Nifula come shortly for the watch.
[*Looking around*] I spy not Ashkenaz.

ASHANTI [*pointing to the King's chamber*]:
Summons has him there.

JABUL: There? Is not the queen within?

ASHANTI:
She hugs her chamber's cloister; will not leave,
I hear, till her petition finds joy.

JABUL:
What shade of summons holds Ashkenaz within?

ASHANTI:
The Book of Memorable Deeds – propped burly
On burly arms for a scribe's ease of view.
If nothing, it keeps the king unpacing,
Who, the livelong night finding no sleep,
Stretched these floors with vigil strolls.

JABUL: I had thought his malady cured.

ASHANTI:
'Tis not his malady; though rambling sore,
His words had not the surge of rage or wrath –
Indeed the queen's gentleness enrobes him.
Why then slumber eluded him eludes us all;
But at dawn, heaving the grand monarch of sighs,
He sent forth Ashkenaz for scribe and book.
What should the Book of Memorable Deeds give him
If not quick summons to lead and lumpen sleep?
Yet the droning drags with bright and open eye.

JABUL:
None I think in Susa tonight found sleep –
Hammers never fell to clamour a Persian night,

Act Five

Or saws so shriek to waste Eastern timber,
As did the flying tools tonight of Haman's hordes.

ASHANTI:
Though not a sound of it within these walls
Was heard, talk of it did filter through.

JABUL:
Mischief stalked the night with evil in tow.

ASHANTI: Is it true 'tis gallows for Mordecai?

JABUL:
It grapples the fearful air like gallows,
But rears a neck to nipple passing clouds –
Can such loftiness boast life to hang one man,
And not be purposed to hoist in harmless quest
A host of spies to the now-neighboured skies?

ASHANTI: Not so towering, surely?

JABUL [*gesturing at his eyes*]:
This veteran pair froze in glimpse; 'tis ready and
    primed;
A monstrous thing, menacing the air,
Scowling wicked thoughts down at Susa.

ASHANTI:
Would some kind soul on wings of swift exile
Away from Persia has sped Mordecai.

JABUL:
Escape, alas, has snatched her face from him,
For Haman, even now, crouches at court
To gain royal leave to use the beast.

ASHANTI:
But what has this Mordecai done to Haman?

KING AHASUERUS [*offstage*]:
But what boon then has this Jew Mordecai received?
[*Enter the King,* ASHKENAZ *and Scribe following.*]

JABUL: Live for ever, King Ahasuerus!

KING AHASUERUS [*to Scribe*]:
What deed in your book more deserves royal boon
Than the act that unclawed the sting of death?
[*He reclines on a couch.*]
I fain would sleep,
Would rest this weary trunk, these hollow eyes,
But night, which came as ever it must,
Brought me nothing, nor rest nor slumber's ease;
And now dawn, like night, greets me with empty hands.
But why? Why in the wake of star-gladness,
This night of sweetest reconciliation,
Does slumber, even rest, escape my breast?
Why, O sleep, have you fled mine eyes?
[*Pause.*]
Mordecai…

Act Five

That name leaps at me with quick and sticking hands!
Once cast off, overthrown by base and lowly thoughts,
When in pomp, with honour sweet and fitting,
He should have been embraced and garland-coiled.
I shame to think on it.
[*To Attendants*]
What shall we do for this Jew Mordecai?
[*Attendants look at one another but remain silent.*]
[*Musing still*]
He's a Jew; a people much maligned, ill-thought of;
Yet did my noble and revered sires,
Great Cyrus, Cambyses, mightiest Darius,
With wit eagle-high above the common herd,
Much favour them – Could I do otherwise?
Could I let their heart, uncovered in the breast
Of this one man Mordecai, go unwrapped, unclothed?
[*To Attendants*] What shall we do for him?
[*Silence.*]
Is there none of rank near, none at court,
Who with fitting counsel may answer me?

JABUL: As I came, O great king,
I did descry Lord Haman at court.

KING AHASUERUS:
Revelling Haman – up this early? Fetch him forth!
                    [*Exit* JABUL.
Good and worthy aide, noble servant.
None in my court counsels better than he.

He revels well, works well, and counsels double well.
He would gladly give me what fleeing sleep,
With malice-fingered snitch, has filched from me:
He would be my brain, ease my mind's perturbation.
[*Pause.*]
'Tis strange, now that I'm resolved to see honour
And royal thanks bestowed on Mordecai,
The garment of heaviness slips my shoulders,
And innocence, sweet friend of sleep, courts me.
I could slumber sleep to shame now, I think.
O night of sweetest reconciliation,
Your reconciliation now is complete and done,
And justice here is born. Does Haman come?

ASHKENAZ: I shall hasten him, my lord.
[*Exit.*

KING AHASUERUS:
'Tis more than relief, this; it tickles me with joy.
Now sleep and joy do sweetly contend...
[*Re-enter* ASHKENAZ.]

ASHKENAZ: My lord,
He comes without my prompting, running hard.

KING AHASUERUS: Loyal and zealous servant!
[*Enter* HAMAN, *followed by* JABUL.]

HAMAN: Live for ever, great king!

Act Five

KING AHASUERUS:
Haman! Breathless on so fair-breathing a morn?

HAMAN:
Where men of lesser love stride with dignity,
Haman divides the air with love's desperate feet.

KING AHASUERUS [*amused*]:
But what business so early brings you to court?

HAMAN:
Ah, my king! The matter I bear the king…
This matter… This matter, my king…

KING AHASUERUS: Haman!

HAMAN: My lord?

KING AHASUERUS: You wear so grave a face,
So grave a face on so fair a day,
And grope and stumble to so grave a voice,
Foretelling too grave a thing; I'll not have graves.

HAMAN: But my lord, this matter –

KING AHASUERUS:
I but think it concerns those… those…

HAMAN: My king?

KING AHASUERUS:
'Tis you should tell me – those you would purge –
Memory hides from me the name you gave.

HAMAN:
There is a man, my king, a certain man…

KING AHASUERUS:
We shall revisit that matter of the purging;
It niggles me unquiet. But leave all now.
Why speak of graves to ears so newly born?
Why darken with gloom eyes that gleam with joy?
But take a gift to clear your face of grief…

HAMAN: A gift for me, my king?

KING AHASUERUS:
Should I not share my gift, what glads my heart,
With one who so oft has gladdened me?

HAMAN: My king, my king…
Were I to go in quest of bounty's own sire,
Where, O king, would I find him but here?
Would I not say, 'Quest, shut your sights elsewhere!
Search no more – here before me stands he!'?

KING AHASUERUS: Do you speak true?

HAMAN: My king!

Act Five

KING AHASUERUS:
I do not stand, I sit, or perhaps do recline.

HAMAN: That he sits or stands,
Nor ever will rust the king's munificence.

KING AHASUERUS:
Yet have I let this matter go to rust.

HAMAN: No, my king, surely not.
This day, truly, is as good a day as any.

KING AHASUERUS:
'Tis an honour I wish to bestow.

HAMAN: But of course, my king –
Though what honour is left the king to give
Does sorely beggar my soul.

KING AHASUERUS:
Drowsiness commands me leave all thinking to you…
Uncover me an honour that honours well
The man the king this day delights to honour.

HAMAN: I shall, my king, I shall.
[*Pause.*]

KING AHASUERUS:
Think fast, lest your labouring mind
Belabours me to laboursome slumber.

HAMAN: My king…

KING AHASUERUS:
I see in your eyes you have it.

HAMAN: I have it, my king; I have it!

KING AHASUERUS: Well?

HAMAN: Will the king not laugh?

KING AHASUERUS: Sleep overwhelms me
And shuts off so happy a thing as mirth.

HAMAN: 'Tis a new-tailored honour; fitting,
Truly fitting, where Honour must burst his robes.

KING AHASUERUS: Well?

HAMAN: Ah, my king…
[*Pause.*]

KING AHASUERUS: Will you not speak?

HAMAN:
'Tis so great! So great! 'Tis a soaring honour!
All eyes will see and know that this favoured one –
This one – truly is the king's chosen!

KING AHASUERUS: My eyelids droop; speak!

HAMAN: Ah…
For this man whom the king delights to honour,
Have a noble prince array him in the king's robes,

In the king's own robes, my lord, in the king's own
    robes…
Ah! … And have this prince lead him through the city
    square
Seated regally on the king's own crowned horse,
The very favoured horse of the king, the king's horse;
Ah! … And as they strut the square to Susa's gaze,
Have the prince with resounding tongue proclaim:
     So shall it be done
To whom the king delights to honour!
     So shall it be done
To whom the king delights to honour!
     So shall it be done
To whom the king delights to honour!

KING AHASUERUS: 'Tis a worthy honour.

HAMAN: Ah, my king,
'Tis the staunchest picture of honour:
Ringing the city with peals of praise,
Fastening all eyes on the king's own chosen!

KING AHASUERUS: It is good.
Now must I to bed; sweet sleep summons me,
And gentle peace lights my way. Now Haman,
As you have counselled, so do for Mordecai –
The Jew who sits at the king's gate. Go now.
Leave nothing out. Conduct the Jew on my horse,
In my robes arrayed with royal splendour;

And with sweet and golden notes trumpet forth
His honouring to Susa's watching eyes.

HAMAN: M-Mordecai?

KING AHASUERUS [*leaving*]:
Sweet morning to you, noble prince;
Wings of joy sweep you on to golden duty!
[*Exit.*
[HAMAN *crumbles to the floor. Guards and Scribe gaze at the spectacle. Lights fade.*]

   Scene 3.—HAMAN'S *house. The living room.*

BILBO *and* SIKURU *laughing to tears.*

BILBO:
Even the stones rocked with laughter –
The sober stones of Persia leapt with mirth!

SIKURU: Nor Susa, nor I, nor all the wine
Of our glad days together, will forget this day!

BILBO:
Did you not see him?
[*In mimicry, chanting it thrice*]
So shall it be done –
To whom the king delights to honour!
[SIKURU *tumbles with laughter.*]

SIKURU: 'Twas his face did trip me!

Act Five

BILBO [*mocking still*]:
So shall it be done –
To whom the king delights to honour!

SIKURU: Humiliation
Never sat so reverent on human face!

BILBO:
And the splinters in his voice spurred the horse
To a rollicking backward-forward merry trot.
Did you not see it?
[*Demonstrating*] So shall it –
Shall it – shall it – shall it –
[*Enter* MIHESO.]

MIHESO: Bilbo,
The royal escorts chafe; come speak with them.
They wear me out with royal mumble.

BILBO:
If the queen would have Haman for her feast
She needs must beg the earth disgorge him.

SIKURU:
'Tis shame to face his court of friends hides him.

BILBO:
Friends? Has the setting sun unveiled any?
When the rib is stripped the vultures hop away,
Nor dawdle a flap for reminding sniff of air.

MIHESO:
What a sparing I was not with you!
I have no stomach for wobbling sights:
He is my master still.

BILBO:
Slush belly! If you, a servant, should heave,
What then should his lady do?

MIHESO:
That it should have been this day she chose
To range and roam the square!

SIKURU:
Better the sight glazed her own eyes, than for Bilbo,
In expounding the sight, to expand it
With lacquer-tongue to unmeasured swelling!

BILBO:
Can any tongue expand this morning's sight?
Did you not see it? So shall it be done
To whom the king delights to honour –
So shall it – shall it – shall it – shall it –
[*They roll with laughter.*]

MIHESO: Yet I would he soon returned –
I dread the blast on him of royal wrath
If longer he hinders the queen's feasting.
[*Enter ZERESH unnoticed. She remains at the doorway, staring blankly.*]

Act Five

SIKURU:
Ah Bilbo! Do you not recall –
Do you not recall once he fell?

BILBO:
'Twas shame and misery gave him two left legs thus –
[*Demonstrates*] So shall it be done –
[*He trips and falls in mockery and they split their sides. At length they notice* ZERESH. *Epitome then of comic catastrophe. They stutter, gulp, choke on wine.* ZERESH *remains silent, staring.* BILBO *and* SIKURU *get stuck trying to hide under the table and have to be freed by* MIHESO. *Old exits are locked and escape is possible only through the door which* ZERESH *occupies. They cringe to the door only to find that* ZERESH *is oblivious of them. They exit, slipping 'through' and around her. After a while* ZERESH *walks into the lounge proper but continues to stare blankly at the audience.*]

HAMAN [*offstage*]:
Zeresh! … Zeresh! … Bilbo!
Where hides the comforting world?
[*He is heard opening and closing doors.*]
Not a friend at court, though well flung in the hour!
Zeresh!
[*He enters.*]
Zeresh!
[*Seeing her*] Zeresh, woe is me…

ZERESH: Woe indeed are you.

HAMAN:
Had I tongue enough to frame description
Of this day, belief yet would shun embrace.

ZERESH: They believe who have not seen,
Should I who have seen and heard not believe?

HAMAN:
You saw? You were there? Oh Zeresh, I'm undone!

ZERESH: Haman, you are undone.

HAMAN: I'm undone!

ZERESH:
You are, Haman! You are undone! You are finished!

HAMAN [*disbelieving*]: Zeresh?

ZERESH: Haman?

HAMAN: Zeresh?

ZERESH: Haman?

HAMAN: What new thing is this?

ZERESH: He was a Jew…

HAMAN: Zeresh?

Act Five

ZERESH: Do you not know
Who they are that bear the name of Jew?

HAMAN:
They themselves know not; should I?
Did you not say –

ZERESH: I said nothing.

HAMAN: The hanging – you counselled…

ZERESH:
Was it not your brain carved it for you?

HAMAN: 'Twas you!

ZERESH: Me?

HAMAN: Zeresh?

ZERESH:
Where are the sons you gave? Where is Vaizatha?
He gives the wind who gives with robbing hands.
[*Pause.*]

HAMAN:
Is this her, who was mine, the maid I married?

ZERESH: The maid you married,
Because you married her, died thirty years ago.

HAMAN: What thing is this?

ZERESH: The end.
[*Pause.*]

HAMAN: Zeresh?

ZERESH:
Thirty years have seen me Haman's fool –
A cistern only for storing Haman's folly,
A vessel for the boast of Haman's pride.
The cistern now has cracked, the vessel smashed,
And the fool of her folly repents.
[*Enter* BILBO.]

BILBO: My master,
The royal escorts to the queen's feast breathe fire.

HAMAN: Is this Zeresh?

ZERESH:
But go! Go heartily to the queen's feast
And return not to crawl these walls for me.
[*Enter* MIHESO.]

MIHESO: Fresh summons from the king arrives…

HAMAN: My ears… My sight…
What burst of darkness now erupts?

ZERESH: You thought to drink the blood of Jew…

Act Five

HAMAN: Was it not you gave me gallows wit?
[*Enter* SIKURU.]

ZERESH: Me?

HAMAN: You counselled…

ZERESH:
I'm a woman – what counsel can a woman give?

SIKURU:
Master, the escorts hold back no longer;
They burst the doors –
[*Enter three royal Escorts.*]

1st ESCORT: Delay no longer, Lord Haman.

2nd ESCORT: The king's temper burns.

3rd ESCORT: We tarry at peril of our lives!
[*They hustle* HAMAN *towards the exit.*]

HAMAN: Zeresh…

ZERESH: Begone!

HAMAN:
What night is this, wraps me cold?
[*Being crowded out*] Zeresh… Zeresh…
             [*Exeunt* HAMAN, *Escorts, Servants.*

Scene 4.—*The palace. The Queen's banquet chamber, which adjoins a small garden visible to the audience.*

Attendants scurry around putting finishing touches to the banquet table. Enter ESTHER, *followed by the King and* HAMAN. *(Guards present.)*

KING AHASUERUS:
And when we waited and saw you not,
We feared some mishap had befallen you.
But what matter made you to your convenience
Stay the queen's pleasure?

HAMAN: My lord?

ESTHER [*to the King*]:
May it please my lord sit here?

KING AHASUERUS: My gracious queen…

ESTHER [*to* HAMAN]:
And may you find pleasure in sitting here.

KING AHASUERUS:
Haman, I hanker after your reply.

HAMAN: My lord?

KING AHASUERUS:
What doom so shadows you, it has stolen your tongue

And given you death's mask for face?
[ESTHER *serves the King wine.*]

ESTHER:
This wine, my king, did from hidden depths teem
   forth.

KING AHASUERUS:
Nor man, nor realm, has known the like of you,
Who though queen, and of beauty fair surpassing,
Thinks nothing to stoop, nor disdains to serve.

ESTHER: My gracious lord.
[*Serving* HAMAN]
The taste of my wine, Haman friend, I vouch
Ever will rest on your tongue.

KING AHASUERUS:
And I but vouch his taciturnity
Is nothing your wine and feast will not cure.
[*To* HAMAN]
Eat, friend; drink and spread with cheer;
Let the queen's delights to the swelling lift you
And with sweet oiling fetch you back your tongue.
And you now, my queen, hold back no longer:
Unclasp your request, lay open your petition.
I have spoken: even my kingdom
To its very half is yours if you ask.

ESTHER [*kneeling before him*]: O great king…

KING AHASUERUS: Speak, my beloved.

ESTHER:
I request nothing but my life, O king,
And petition naught but rescue for my people.
[*Silence.*]

KING AHASUERUS: Is this request or jest?

ESTHER: My people and I
Into the fierce furnace of death are thrust!
[*Pause.*]
Nor slavery, nor chains, nor threat of pain,
Could move me assail the king's repose;
Naught could to this move me but heat of death
From blaze of genocide. A genocide, my king,
Which smoulders now to consume my people.

KING AHASUERUS: Genocide…

ESTHER:
I stand in plea with life consigned to death.

KING AHASUERUS: You? Who could dare?

ESTHER: There stands he!
[*Silence.*]

KING AHASUERUS: Haman?

Act Five

ESTHER [*to* HAMAN]:
Give report to the king, chief minister,
Of your plot, the lot you cast for Jewish death.
Recount your wish to rid the earth of Jew,
Your plot to slay, annihilate, destroy –
To have the Jew from earth erased! – tell him!

KING AHASUERUS: Jew – you?

ESTHER: Your handmaid, O king, is Jew –
Plotted to the death, condemned by this man,
This wicked Haman, foe and enemy!

KING AHASUERUS: No…
[*He rises, toppling the table's fare, and storms off to the garden.*]

HAMAN: Aiee! It has come to this!

ESTHER:
There's ever a day of reckoning, friend;
Ever will judgment come.

HAMAN: Aiee! I'm undone!
[*He rises and staggers to* ESTHER.]
Plead for me! If you plead for me…

ESTHER:
Let the hands strong and able to cast the lot
Be the hands strong and able to plead for you.

HAMAN: O my queen! I beg of you…

ESTHER: Away!

HAMAN: Help me, my queen!

ESTHER: Who was it shot the arrow
That in warped flight bends always to return?

HAMAN: O my queen! O my queen!

ESTHER: Away from me, enemy of the Jews!
[*She walks away from him and reclines on a couch. But he comes to her and in desperation flings himself at her.*]

HAMAN:
My lady, I beg of you! I beg of you!
Plead for me!

ESTHER: Unhand me! Lay off!
[*The King returns.*]
Lay off! Away!

KING AHASUERUS: What!

HAMAN: Aiee! I'm undone!

KING AHASUERUS [*to Guards*]: Seize him!
[*Guards rush to seize* HAMAN.]

HAMAN: Mercy, O king! Mercy!

Act Five

KING AHASUERUS:
Within my own walls, before my eyes?

HAMAN: Mercy! Aiee! Mercy!

KING AHASUERUS [*to Guards*]:
Death to the fiend!

HAMAN: No, my king! No! Aiee!
[*Guards force a hood over* HAMAN'S *head.*]

KING AHASUERUS: My ring!
[*The King's signet ring is ripped off* HAMAN'S *finger, and* HARBONA *returns it to the King who wears it.*]

HAMAN [*being dragged off*]: Aiee! Aiee! Aiee!
　　　　　　　　[*Exeunt Guards with* HAMAN.

HARBONA:
O just king, standing now by Haman's house
Is the gallows Haman built for the hanging
Of Mordecai the Jew whose word saved the king.

KING AHASUERUS: Feed it!

HARBONA: As you command, my king.
　　　　　　　　　　　　[*Exit.*

ESTHER: Allow me soothe my lord's brow...

KING AHASUERUS: He dared assault you!

ESTHER: Soft, my king; soft…

KING AHASUERUS: The treacherous fiend!

ESTHER:
With him perishes his hanging device
On my father. But soft, my king…

KING AHASUERUS: Your father…

ESTHER:
Who was to me a father – Mordecai.

KING AHASUERUS: Mordecai?

ESTHER:
If ever a child had a father, 'twas he.
When death was quick to name me orphan, Mordecai,
Valiant cousin, was swift to call death liar;
And with arms spilling with sweet nurturing
Did raise me full in love's abundance,
That when I looked on him, as ever I did,
I saw in that one face, in that one frame,
The father and mother I never knew,
And out of his rolling laughter would come
The brothers and sisters my child's heart sought.

KING AHASUERUS: Esther…
[*They embrace.*]
Was it you, even you, I doubted?
[*Presently to Attendants*]

Act Five

Fetch forth the queen's father!
Usher the noble Jew Mordecai before me.
                              [*Exeunt Attendants.*
[*To* ESTHER]
Wherefore made you so kernelled a secret
Of this good thing?

ESTHER:
I was caught and bound by secrecy's chains.
The life of Jew within these palace walls
Mordecai feared was worth a fig, no more;
Therefore did I, locked in the gatherer's net,
Hold myself in vow to hide race and kin.

KING AHASUERUS:
Even in death's face you would hold your vow?

ESTHER:
I had sworn, my king, as sure as I'm sworn
To your bed alone. Nor did I know release
Till bidden to intercede for my race.

KING AHASUERUS:
My noble wife, jewelled pure to the last…
[ESTHER *falls at his feet.*]
Esther, no! … No! … Rise…
Rise to my bosom and there ever cling,
My Esther, my jewel, my queen… Come now…
You weep! Wherefore… Why? Why, Esther, why?

ESTHER:
My people are tented still in death's fields.

KING AHASUERUS: Ah...
[*Enter* MORDECAI *ushered in by Attendants, with* HARBONA *returning.*]

ESTHER: Papa...

MORDECAI [*prostrating*]: My king! My queen!

KING AHASUERUS:
Rise, Mordecai, beloved sire, or Esther,
Lately barred from comradeship with the floor,
Shall find no father's arms to weep in. Rise, sire!
[*To* ESTHER]
Why hold back? His arms beg your due.

ESTHER: Papa... Papa...
[ESTHER *and* MORDECAI *fly into each other's arms.*]

KING AHASUERUS [*watching*]: Fall softly, tears;
Sweet showers of love's reunion, flow soft...

HARBONA [*approaching the King*]:
Your command is done, O king, and Haman strung.

KING AHASUERUS: How high hangs he?

HARBONA:
The highest a hanging ever will see, O king!

Act Five

KING AHASUERUS:
'Tis well. Let his corpulence call the kites
To ripe and lofty feast, bowing necks that peck,
Bending knees that claw, if so it pleases his highness.
[*Pause. The King approaches the embracing two.*]
Now to embrace you, lace you heart-close,
Fount and father of my sweetest joy!
[*He and* MORDECAI *embrace. The King pulls off his signet ring.*]
Wear this – my signet ring, seal of authority.

MORDECAI: My king?

KING AHASUERUS:
'Tis yours to hold and use on my behalf.

MORDECAI:
Your meaning, O king, alights not upon my brow.

KING AHASUERUS:
Would you bid me look elsewhere? At your post,
Lowly at the gates, you served me close,
Your heart near, your eyes keener than courtier's
Or any prized and loyal chamberlain's;
Now, arise; ascend on wings the summit.
Cast your gaze on the land and loose your heart
Upon my outstretched regions to do for all
What so well you did for your king.
[*To* ESTHER]
Counsel of my heart, my fount of prudence,

Who better to be the chief minister
Our paired wisdom pronounced fitting ever I have?

ESTHER:
I know none, nor have known any, my king,
More able than this man my father.

KING AHASUERUS: Uttered and settled;
Yes, be seated, my chief minister; do sit.
Surprise, like fatigue, quick to the sitting
Oft will wrestle the strongest haunches.
Now tell me, good sire, father of my bride,
When will you appraise your daughter's estate?

ESTHER:
May it please the king, of what estate speaks he?

KING AHASUERUS: Of my fair Esther's estate.

ESTHER: My estate?

KING AHASUERUS:
All Haman's estate, second only to the king's
As prize, now is yours. Riches vaster by far
Than the boast in the realm of any man
Or conquered king: All that is yours, Esther,
To use and dispose as your heart wills,
Without first or ever briefing the king.

Act Five

ESTHER: My lord and king…
[*Pause.*]

KING AHASUERUS:
But I do discern that your face, Esther,
Yet lacks joy, has only the shadow of it,
A fleeting thing that comes in hopping perches
And flaps off, disdaining to primp its nest.
'Tis the edict, the annihilation command –
It yet hacks at you? Ah, Esther…

ESTHER:
My lord knows my heart; revoke the edict, O king,
And invoke me joy to stay.

KING AHASUERUS:
You know, Esther, that an edict in the king's name,
With signet ring sealed, cannot be revoked;
You know this well, yet you know me not…

ESTHER:
I know my lord is king, and my king
Is not without power to find means
To encamp joy in his queen's sorrowing tents.

KING AHASUERUS:
Why be sorrowed then? I would have this day,
In this matter in which your desire
Straddles my will, given you without your plea
The gift of your heart's pining. So let it be:

If we cannot revoke the past, can we not
Like the morn born anew, decree us a new day?
Therefore speed forth in my name a new edict
Heaping on the Jew the tide of golden favour.
With my ring cast your word strong in iron,
Pronouncing what ridge and rock beseem your cause.
Mordecai my chief minister, what word should blaze?
Should word not muster the Jew to fend off threats
As shield gleamed to piercing by royal shine?
Should word not motion the Jew to raise sword
By royal stone honed to the dread of smiting foe?
Esther, who from the king draws all she desires,
What word should blaze? Should word not froth
    command –
Such as would brim your heart with lasting joy?
Ah, my Esther, the radiance of your smile
Wears the glow and gold of the risen sun.
Beauty bereft of smile is fallen flower –
But now my rose with breath of dew blooms anew.
To work then! To work! Let the scribes attend!
Work the edict to the loud swell of joy!
Streak the realm with couriers on lightning rides
In thundering din blaring the Jew's deliverance!
Today, this day, is the Jew delivered!
Mordecai, but you have my seal… Esther… Come…
Let your king closely look upon your smile.

ESTHER:
My king, what name this day shall bear!

Act Five

KING AHASUERUS [*to* MORDECAI]:
My prince, has silence named you hers?

MORDECAI:
May the king indulge me my clammed lips;
What but silence's fortress can hold joy's tempest?
What unnumbed heart can hold the avalanche of joy,
This storm of gladness, that since this day began
Has joined with a hand unseen to roll me down?

KING AHASUERUS:
Only to roll you up again –
Up with me, my prince, is where you belong.
But now I shall be your lips. Harbona!

HARBONA:
Your command, great and noble king!

KING AHASUERUS:
Wait not for the edict; escape the news –
What you have heard and seen – burst all forth!
Let the criers cry the city hoarse,
Gushing these tidings at the head of every street.
Let the city clap its hands and Susa rejoice!
Let all of goodwill exult this day! Go!

HARBONA:
With dancing heart and merry heels, my king.
                                              [*Exit.*

KING AHASUERUS: Esther…

ESTHER:
Happiness raids my soul like music;
My heart, my soul, my very flesh, break out in song!

KING AHASUERUS [*to Attendants*]:
Call the chamberlains, the courtiers! Let all rejoice!
This day has salvation come to Jewish breast!
Rejoice! Rejoice! Let all who breathe rejoice,
For this day has the Jew known salvation!
O happy day! Rejoice! Rejoice! Rejoice!
[*Lights fade.*]

The End

About the author

Philip Begho is the author of several award-winning books. His wide-ranging interest has seen him in a varied career that has spanned journalism, banking, business, legal practice and university teaching. He has also engaged in film and theatrical production.

He now works as a full-time writer, concentrating largely on children's literature and verse drama.